FISHING WELL

IS THE

BEST REVENGE

Stories About Boats, Fishing, Friends,
Captains, Oregon Inlet,
and Fishing the Mid-Atlantic

Written by Jeff Waxman
Edited and Foreword by Elliott Stark

ISBN 978-1-62806-283-0 (print | paperback)

Library of Congress Control Number 2020910217

Published by Salt Water Media
29 Broad Street, Suite 104
Berlin, MD 21811
www.saltwatermedia.com

Cover images used courtesy of the author.
Cover design by Salt Water Media.
Editing by Elliott Stark.

FISHING WELL

IS THE

BEST REVENGE

TABLE OF CONTENTS

Section 2: Lessons From Boats and Fishing

FOREWORD

When Jeff Waxman called me to ask about editing a book of fishing stories, I must admit I was at first a bit skeptical. Books of stories can be a hard thing to sell. Without the name recognition of an industry icon or the distribution channels associated with established brands, it can be difficult to persuade people to buy a book (at least enough of them to make publishing one an economic endeavor). Besides, these days do people even read books anymore? And if you were to consume some entertaining stories, shouldn't they be published on the internet for *free*? You get the picture.

As I thought about our initial conversation, I began thinking about the prospect. I knew Jeff to be a very nice guy. Besides, I had taken plenty of odd jobs that were odder than this one (and I've even tried to sell things with less hope of success). So, after a bit of thought I figured working with Mr. Waxman on a book of fishing stories might be something good to do. I figured that worst case, it would be a good excuse to go fishing a couple of times.

When I called Jeff to let him know that I was in, I expressed my concerns about fishing stories. We get stories submitted to *In The Bite Magazine* often enough that I've learned to recognize the pitfalls of the genre. Stories should have takeaways... they should provide either some kind of lesson or impart some kind of meaningful experience. Most of the time, they don't.

Another thing that worried me about fishing stories was the tendency of many writers to turn out tales that are in fact little more than thinly veiled catch statistics buttered up by a cliché or two and a couple of catch phrases. Another classic is the use of a story to forcefully tell people how good you are at fishing, while making them read how funny you are. The ego trip might be worse than the catch report.

I also related the importance of having an anchor point. After all, for stories to be impactful they must first have a foundation to which others can relate. Otherwise, you're writing science fiction or fantasy or something.

So of course, I told Jeff and his wonderful wife Eileen about these reservations before reading anything. After all, it is the mind uncluttered and without bias that reasons best, I reasoned. It was only then that I got to the stories...

I read the first two late one night. I laughed a lot. I couldn't wait to read the others. My favorite of the bunch is "The Best Fishing Story Never Told." My wife heard me laughing from the other room. "What are you cackling about in there," she asked.

The stories are great. Not only are they imminently relatable, but many of them happened at a time and in a place that may one day be remembered like something of a fishing version of Renaissance Florence. Jeff was fortunate enough to come of fishing age during the glory days of Oregon Inlet. He was there when the Buddy Davises and Omie Tilletts of the world were transforming forever what the world wanted from a sportfishing boat.

How close was Jeff to the action? He owned Buddy Davis hull number one. The captain? None other than a young Bull Tolson. From the fishing to the ways of the world, it was a different time-- one never to be experienced again.

This book is a hilarious collection of stories written in such a way as to be inviting to partake in this time-- and a few times before and since. I once read somewhere that for someone to be able to write a story suitable for enjoyment by others, that person must like people. Whoever wrote this continued that, were a person to not like the world around him, it would bleed through his or her words, tainting them. Even if I hadn't spent quite a bit of time working with him, I'd wager that Jeff enjoys his life and the people with whom he shares it. It is evident in his stories.

From inadvertently providing material for a bus load of Japanese scrap bookers in the Virgin Islands to the lifelong lessons imparted to an impetuous young fisherman by a New York charter captain, to a drunk, naked chick dancing her way onto a Coast Guard vessel while under tow, this is a collection of stories worth reading. They are certainly worth an afternoon of your time—maybe the next time your fishing is blown out.

- Elliott Stark

INTRODUCTION

Like lots of kids, I was always fascinated by water, boats and fishing. While this condition strikes many young children, in my case it got worse over time. My career in business was punctuated by this fascination. My life has been annotated by the sea...

Diving for lobsters off of the New Jersey coast paid for much of my college education. I taught scuba diving in Thailand during the Vietnam conflict. Looking back, I've done lots of things related to the ocean, but it was my first marlin trip out of Cape Hatteras in 1972 that was perhaps most impactful.

This trip began a love of offshore fishing, Carolina boats and the entire offshore experience... Since 1972 I've been hooked! This infatuation has many metrics. It is measured chiefly in fish caught and boats owned. Just how many boats? Many...Formula 233F, Marauder, Boston Whaler, Ray Hunt 30' Tournament Fish, Buddy Davis 46' Hull #1, several Center consoles, etc...currently 35' Donzi Center Console offshore rigged.

There is as much to love about coastal North Carolina as there are stories about the place. Hatteras, Oregon Inlet, The Oregon Inlet Fishing Center. Big rigs, single engines—all manner of boat, anything to get after the world class fishing. And then there are the captains and mates...all somehow melding together to form an interesting and intriguing world.

Since my first foray into the mix in the early 70s, I've had the privilege of watching the transformation. Boats have come a long way... from the old canoe-sterned rigs running 15 knots to the "proud bow" of Warren O'Neal, Omie Tillett and Buddy Davis. How fascinating it has been.

Not to be outdone by the size and complexity of the vessels

themselves, the power inside the boats is something once unimaginable. *The Gal O Mine*, with her 12v71Ti, cruised in the mid 20 knot range...and held together! It was Game On! Speeds grew, size grew...the latest advertisement for Spencer Sportfish promises 45 knot...cruise!

While the boats that come out of this part of North Carolina have literally changed the fishing world, the underlying stories of the people and times were the fascinating parts. I had the good fortune to know many of the boys and am pleased to share many of the stories. They are all true, in no particular order, just fun...hopes that you enjoy.

- Jeff Waxman

Oregon Inlet: The Early Days!

It was June 1971 and I was freshly back from the Vietnam War. I returned to my job as Salesman for Office Equipment Company (Xerox Corp). Fishing paid for much of college (in the form of proceeds from diving for lobsters off the Jersey Coast) and was my vocation in the Service (teaching scuba in Thailand). It just so happened that fishing also became a frequent topic of discussion between my Boss and me.

To my pleasant surprise, he one day invited me on a marlin fishing trip to NC... We were headed to Cape Hatteras to fish on the *Early Bird* with Captain Emory Dillon. It was a good thing that the run was short, as the *Early Bird* (later to become the Stormy Duchess) was a solid 16 knots! Our mate that day? None other than Chip Shafer (later to become a famous, influential and highly skilled captain in his own right). It was quite a start for a kid who thought bluefish were a big deal!

Emory set up in 50 fathoms. I was quite impressed at being able to actually see the baits as we trolled. Before we hit the 100 mark, we had a white one hooked up...my first time ever billfish! After a 15 minute fight, came the release. It was success and it happened before 8:00am.

Then came the dolphin. If memory serves, we boated a half dozen including one nice bull, before all Hell broke loose. The mate started running around, the Captain was yelling this rigger or that. Somehow, out of what seemed to my novice offshore fishing eyes to be chaos, we shortly had our blue one hooked up.

Watching my boss on the fish I was spellbound! After a short fight, Chip billed and released the fish-- all 180-200 or so pounds of him. Emory came off the bridge to cut the line at the hook. It was a great day.

After thanking Emory and Chip, we drove sixty miles north from Hatteras to Oregon Inlet. The second day of my first trip was on the *Mel O Dee* run by Capt. Buddy Cannady (later to become a world class boat builder) with mate Billy McAskill (who went on to own WhaleBone Tackle). It was another good day. We missed two whites but boated dozen or more dolphin, with one bull close to forty pounds. I was hooked...deep!

I had heard of Hatteras before but Oregon Inlet was new to me. The fishing in Oregon Inlet was as good, maybe better, than Hatteras. The accommodations were much better and Oregon Inlet was also closer to my home and work in Northern Virginia.

I began to spend all of my free time there. Soon I bought a beach house and boats...several...and became a regular offshore. Without knowing it at the time, we were involved in what may have been the beginnings of the glory days of Oregon Inlet.

What made Oregon Inlet so special? It was more than the fishing—it was the people. For context, consider some of the names of the men involved. A common trend among them is transition, and the need to describe how they started and what they went on to do. Capt. Chip Shafer, began his career working in the cockpits of men like Emory Dillon. He has gone on to run sportfishers around the world. Many of the men who worked with him, similarly, have gone on to be the headliners of the modern age of sportfishing captains. Chip was far from alone in being a young man involved in these stories who would go on to leave a lasting and influential legacy on the world of fishing.

Buddy Davis was a mate before he ran the *Fish N Fool*. That was until he became the best known of the original Carolina boat builders. Davis and several others helped popularize the Carolina Flare. The "proud bow" that took head seas better than any boat anywhere and has, a few decades later, become a signature from this part of the world.

Billy Holton also was building boats. He was building his 50 foot *Fireball*. Bright red and fast, she was one of the queens of the fleet.

Paul Spencer was another charter captain at the time. He was learning the boat building skills and trade from father-in-law, Sheldon Midgette — himself a Carolina charter captain. Omie Tillett, captain of *The Sportsman*, also began building boats. Tillet learned many of his skills from working with Warren O'Neal...himself the original builder of the Carolina look! (I spent a full blow day watching Warren tar a teak cockpit in the *Jeannie*. It was quite an experience). Sonny Briggs, now one of the boat builders, was running the *Bishop II* at the time—all the while learning the how and why of the trade himself.

Of course Ricky Scarborough was there too. He was building in a shed in Wanchese right beside Buddy Davis! I watched him build the 40' *Wild Card*, one of the first express boats in memory.

Paul Mann, up the road in Manns Harbor, was creating boats of beauty too. Mann built the 57' *Magic Marlin* for friend John Evans. I believe it was the first big rig that I fished on with 30 knot cruise... in 1998!

Buddy Cannady went from the 34' *Mel O Dee* to Davis hull #1, the *Capt BC*. Immediately after his switch, Cannady himself began building boats. He started by building one per year, fishing it then selling it to build another. Cannady's transition turned out quite helpful for me, as I bought the Davis hull #1 from BC himself.

John Bayliss ran the *Tarheel*, a 46' Scarborough boat, with mate Marty Brill before he began to build. In fact, I came close to buying the *Tarheel* from John in 1981. Once his operation grew to what it has become, John bought the Scarborough boat back and refinished it. He now runs it out of Los Sueños in Costa Rica. She is beautiful and wins tournaments! Sometimes, when describing the make of the boat, magazines refer to the Tarheel as a Scarborough/Bayliss boat.

Thinking back on these early years there are several points that come to mind. What follows are the takeaways that are important enough to articulate:

1. **Every single one of the guys noted above, like every other captain fishing then in Oregon Inlet who is not mentioned, shared information with each other...freely.** Sure, everyone competed, but everyone helped each other. This freedom of information was extended to those of us with private boats (both big and small) as well. If we called a charter captain, the call was returned. They shared locations of schools of dolphin, what baits to use, numbers—all kinds of things. Private boats would

reciprocate. I strongly believe that this willingness to work together was a necessary component of what made Oregon Inlet successful beyond compare.

2. Boats were built for the seas they fished, and 90% of them had single engines. The reasoning behind the single screw is easy. Single engines are less weight, burn less fuel, are less maintenance, and cost less than double engines. These are important considerations when your boat is also your livelihood.

Most boats fished the same areas so if an issue arose there was company (although once a diesel starts at the dock it generally runs all day). Another of the central attributes to most of the vessels was dictated by the physical setting they fished. Given the need to "cross the bar" daily, with occasional heavy seas and shoal waters, most boats were built with full keels and protected running gear. In case of touching bottom, damage was averted by the build.

3. The fleet in Oregon Inlet fished hard. It also fished in most seas. Oregon Inlet captains fished in seas that would be considered blow days in many ports. They fished until 2:30 or when the box (stern mounted always!) was full. The captains here put limits on catches before limits became laws. The dolphin boat limit was a prime example. Beyond simply fishing hard and fishing for themselves, the captains here tried to make sure that the fleet did well, realizing that the world sees them as a whole far more so than just individuals.

4. And lastly, one can never forget the Morning Prayer! I believe it began in the early 70's, started by and orated daily by Omie Tillett. It was always a thing of beauty. The morning prayer was part religious appeal to the Lord to protect and care for the men and the Fleet; part community update noting who was in need and the things needing to be done. We all looked forward to hearing Omie begin in his Elizabethan dialect, "Dee Er Law Erd..." Even today when fishing elsewhere, I give a mental morning prayer to the guys and the boats on their way offshore.

When thinking back on the Oregon Inlet of the 1970's and early 80's, thoughts are filled with both fishing and friendships. Each, both the fishing and the friendships, were as good as they get. These are fond memories, ones that are still savored.

Oregon Inlet 2020

Fast forward to today. The world of charter captains building a single boat over the winter has changed dramatically and unalterably. The world of single engine, full-keel charter style rigs has morphed. The landscape of sport fishing will never be the same. The 42-46 foot rigs of factory boats have been replaced by custom rigs, many built by former Oregon Inlet captains.

These custom boats are the nexus of money, taste and boat building. The skill and craftsmanship (not to mention the quality (and price) of the materials involved) have never been seen before. All of this, from the millionaire owners to the imported plywoods and the meetings with fisherman-turned-boatbuilders, somehow comes together in this tiny little fishing port.

With the notable exception of Viking, most of the top guns today have boats built by Paul Spencer or John Bayliss or Paul Mann — all guys who know the seas from working the cockpit to the helm. The boats are drop dead gorgeous, generally 60 feet and up, fully equipped and ready to fish the world. Modern boats are commonly equipped with cruise speeds of 35 knots plus, fuel capacities often in excess 2000 gallons, interiors finer than the finest homes... often built from a single tree trunk to assure matching grains.

Fishing boats that could well be museum pieces come with everything you could ever want — tackle storage, etched glass, the finest leathers, televisions that recede into cabinetry when not in use. What passes for the "normal complement of freezers and a galley" these days would suit the gourmet chef.

These days custom Carolina boats are found all over the world. From Cape Verde, throughout the Caribbean, Costa Rica, Hawaii, Australia...to name but a few locations. And they continue to get better and faster. Bayliss' latest 62' Gameboat has 41 knot cruise. Spencer's newest will be water jet powered — cruising in excess of 45 knots, topping out over 50 knots! These were the speeds to make the go fast crowd happy just a few years ago.

If all of that were not amazing enough, check out some of these boats that are being sold on the used market today. Some go for more than were paid for new! That is something that at one point in time would have been unimaginable.

The big boat sport fishing world has been turned upside down in the last ten years. This transformation was brought not by Bertram nor by Hatteras, but as a result of the early days of the Oregon Inlet Charter Captains. Far from aiming to change the sportfishing world forever, these were men who wanted boats to get out and back safely, quickly and in comfort, to cross the bar, bring in a day's catch and do it again the next day and the next.

Yep, Oregon Inlet, my old stomping grounds, has changed boats and boat building forever. There is no doubt that this revolution can be traced to boats being built by captains, not by factories nor by corporations. Believe it... These men are the best fishing fleet and boat builders in the world!

Section 1:

Oregon Inlet

THE BIG ONE
(THAT GOT AWAY)

It all started with meeting a guy with his new 28' Bertram in 1974. He was at my marina and staring at the outriggers on my boat. My ride at the time was a 23' Formula 233F. The boat was rigged for offshore, powered with twin Holman Moody Ford 235s (I've always had need for speed).

Finally, after the staring came the questions...What are riggers for? Then there were the questions about tackle and the "where, how, whens of fishing." We became friends over time and in '75 we ran his boat from Northern Virginia to fish Oregon Inlet for two weeks.

We hired a local freelance mate to help us out. He was there to rig baits, provide local knowledge, and played a role common to traveling outfits like ours. We set out with our Penn Senators (114H's if memory serves) and my pride and joys...two new 50 Internationals on brown Fenwick sticks. The weather was good and we fished The Point for four days. We did well; we caught dolphin, yellowfin, wahoo. It was great fishing and a fun time.

On the fifth day of the trip, our mate suggested we try running north instead in hopes of a blue marlin. He rigged squids, mackerel and a huge swimming mullet. We were ready.

We ran northeast before setting out in forty fathoms. We had five head on the boat, I was at the helm. We decided to put out five lines — one for each of us. I was last and got the left long with the big swimming mullet, rigged with a two ounce chin weight.

The first four lines were out and set. Next we dropped back my mullet. Within minutes, I saw a huge purple shadow under my bait. I grabbed the rod. As the fish engulfed the bait, I dropped back straight into the mouth of a blue one far bigger than I could comprehend...

Its mouth looked like the opening of a fifty gallon oil drum. She was scary big! I dropped back for as long as I could stand, before moving the drag to strike. The hook found its mark and out of the water came a monster of a blue marlin. The fight began. We hooked up at 9:15am.

Attached to the monster, I managed to get into the chair. For the first three or four hours we basically chased the fish. The sea was flat calm. Most of the line I gained was due to boat backing down on or running with the fish. To say it was a standoff would be giving me more credit than due-- the fish was running the show!

Sometime around midafternoon, the fish slowed then stopped running. We gained much line it had taken during the first part of the fight.

After the fish stopped running, I felt the line bump hard two or three times. We thought the sharks were on the fish so we got as close to the fish as we could-- within maybe twenty yards or so. The water was crystal clear.

Looking over the side, there were no sharks but there is our fish in midst of a school of small bonito. The bumping was several bonito hitting the line. Unless my mind and eyes deceived me, there was my hooked up monster marlin, chasing and eating the small tuna-like fish...while hooked and pulling twenty pounds of drag!

Soon the marlin moved off and the fight was back on. At this point, we were maybe six hours in. I was tired, sunburnt and my shoulders were bleeding from where the harness was digging into them. My feet hurt from pressure. She was winning....!

Given the state of the angler at this point, I told the crew we had to try and take her. I figured the fish was likely a 50-pound record (for records to be valid, only the angler can touch the rod), and that our best approach was to get the flyer ready and give it our best shot.

Time and time again, she would settle, we would get close enough to grab the leader (#15 wire — in those days we used single strand) 15 feet double line and 15 feet leader. She'd burn off maybe 50 yards and we'd try again. Again and again this went, for two hours...same give and take.

I was getting whipped and we were not winning. We did this dance maybe 30, maybe 40 times... Did we begin to make headway? We thought so.

Finally at 5:30, the mate got the wire. He managed to get his feet up under the covering boards and was firmly locked in, ready to do battle. I jumped up and grabbed the flying gaff...no one else on the boat had any idea of what to do. The mate held on, I had the flyer cleated off and ready to strike. Just them the fish jumped and tailwalked beside the boat-- just out of reach of the gaff...

And the wire broke right at the corner of the jaw. It just gave out! Freed up, she jumped again, seemed to shake herself then grey-hounded for 50 yards before disappearing.

Stunned, speechless, totally beat....nobody spoke for maybe 10 minutes...there was nothing to be said. She won, hands down, no doubt, she won.

Me? Exhausted, burnt, feet and shoulders bloodied.... She won.

While my physical appearance would have been simple enough to describe, the emotional response to the situation was very complex. I was dejected about losing the fish of a lifetime, sure. Aside and apart from the dejection, I was also quietly elated...for the majesty, the purity, the beauty of such a phenomenal animal. To see and be part of such an experience was life changing. To this day, some 44 years later, I'm still captivated (and owned by in a way) by that day.

I am also profoundly thankful to have had my chance. She won.

*** Of course, the question comes up… "Just how big was she?!" We will never know of course. Of the five of us on the boat, only the mate and I had any experience…the other three guys had no context.

I offer only the following….the mate said she was a grander. My guess that day was 900ish. "That day" is important to note because three days later we boated a 546 pound blue marlin, which by comparison looked small! Small!

In reality, no guess really matters. If I had to say it, she probably was well over the grander mark…maybe even bigger than she looks in my imagination today.

God bless that fish!

Where We At, Hoss?

The fishing trip began easily enough. We planned a two week stay in the Oregon Inlet Fishing Center on my buddy's 28' Bertram. It was early 1975, we booked a slip for two weeks and ran the boat down from Virginia. The boat owner was relatively inexperienced so the original idea was to hire a freelance mate for the entire two weeks. Yours truly would run the boat and the owner and/or other friends would be the anglers. And it went according to plan…mostly!

The first days were glorious, calm seas, great fishing. It was as good as it gets…we were having a great time. The boat owner was a small man, desperate to learn and understand as much about the sea and fishing as could get. By this time, given that I am about 275 pounds, he's nicknamed me "Hoss"…a takeoff on the old TV series about the Cartwrights. Our mate was a local guy, young and anxious to show well. And he brought his girlfriend when we had room.

On or about the end of the first week, two bits intersected to create a very memorable experience. **Bit one:** The boat owner tells me that he "wants to be the Captain" the next day. After discussion (much!) and given the next day's forecast of flat calm, I reluctantly agreed. Given his newly minted title for the next day, he wanted me to guarantee that he would get no help. He was to be the Captain and, no matter what, if he asked anything, I was to say "It's up to the Captain".

Bit two: One of the charter boats at the dock needed a mate for the day. Our guy asked if we would mind him going with the charter if he made us a cooler of baits...AND, if so would we mind taking his girlfriend out with us without him. We agreed to both....!

Note that in the day our "electronics" package consisted of a manual RDF (radio direction finder), a round flashing depth finder, twin 215 HP gas engines carrying a single fuel tank of 180 gallons. A CB radio and a newly installed VHF completed our complement. Clearly, there were limitations to be considered!

At first light the next day, we head out following the fleet. The main body of boats was generally heading to the 630 line to target tuna. The 630 was 32 miles from the dock—pretty close to the limit for us.

Several boats, however, kept going all the way to and past the Tower. This body of boats was running about 45-48 miles before setting out. They were marlin fishing, not tuna fishing. And he followed them! Fuel was about to become a problem.

Fishing was good-- dolphin, wahoo, blue one window shopping, and the seas flat calm. The mate's girlfriend spent most of the day napping or in the bow in a bikini. She was pretty, shapely and good company. Not only that, but she was happy to make sandwiches.

By about 2:00pm, we had enough fuel to make it back most of the way. It was becoming clear, however, that we did not have enough to guarantee we wouldn't risk crossing the bar on fumes. At 2:30, the charters picked up. My Captain, however, wanted to stay for another hour...all the while trolling offshore yet further.

When 3:30 comes around we pick up. The owner heads into the cabin and comes out white as a sheet. "Hoss, do we have enough fuel to get home?"

I answer, "I dunno, ask the Captain!"

This goes on for a few minutes until he reaches panic stage. "Hoss, what are we gonna do?"

Well, we now have a serious discussion. I tell him that, 1) We will be maybe 10-15 miles short of fuel at cruising speed so do not run hard, and; 2) Once in range we call the Coast Guard for help (in those days they came to get you, tow you to the fuel dock and treat you nicely all the while). So, that's what we did.

At maybe 15 miles out the Coast Guard met us. Aboard were three guys — two young guys and a heavyset old Bosun's Mate on the helm. The Coasties hook up the tow line and help us back to the dock. Still flat calm, it was now the early evening of a gorgeous day.

By now, unbeknownst to the rest of us, our mate's girlfriend had found the vodka...and was clearly inebriated. As we approached the bar, she heads out to the bow...the Eagles latest tape is on the stereo...turned on full volume...and she begins to dance! She gets way into her dance, takes her top off and we're all wondering what's next. Now, the Coasties tell us to shorten the tow line as we cross the bar, which we do.

She continues to dance...topless...while the two young guys are transfixed. The old guy, trying not to look, is hanging on to the helm and looking forward. One of the young guys yells, "Take your bottom off!"

She yells back, "Only if you take your hat off!"

Our now naked dancer is gyrating to "All I Need Is The Air That I Breathe" when the Coasties ask if she will jump on to their boat-- which she does! Upon boarding the Coast Guard vessel, she immediately pulls down the pants of the Bosuns Mate...under which he is wearing huge dark green Vietnam style boxer shorts. And it gets more interesting....much more.

The Coast Guard tows us to the fuel dock. Their crew is now dressed and appearing sheepish, but happy. All is well. The owner decides not to be the Captain any longer, our mate is available for the next day....there is joy in Mudville....

Mid-day the next day as I'm on the bridge, the VHF crackles to life. It's the Oregon Inlet Coast Guard... calling my boat. Nervously, I pick up.

"This is the OI Coast Guard, Captain. We are calling to see if you need anything today, if so we'll be happy to bring it out to you!"

Way back in the day...

Wood and Glue

Since the late 70s and generally to this day, most of the Oregon Inlet charter fleet run big, single engine boats outfitted with Carolina flare. Some are equipped with full keels... there is lots of shoal water, after all. Shoal water being the local term for the many shallow, generally unmarked sandbars that are known to shift widely.

The reasoning behind outfitting their boats in this way is simple. Once running, the diesel engine generally runs until shut down. A single is much less complicated than twins and (since most boats are captain-owned and hence support the family) burn much less fuel. A typical trip offshore may well burn 130 - 150 gallons while running 32-35 miles and trolling all day. Oil changes and maintenance are halved compared to twin engine boats. And besides, all of the local Captains can handle the single better than most of us can with twins and thrusters!

Buddy Davis began his career on the water working on charter boats. An experienced charter captain running the *Fish n Fool*, Buddy built hull number one of what would become Davis Yachts for Captain Buddy Cannady. Cannady (himself to later become a renowned NC boat builder), christened the boat the the *Capt BC*!

If memory serves correctly, BC ran the Davis hull for two years. He then built his own boat and offered the Davis hull to me to run as a charter after I expressed interest. The boat was fully rigged, powered by a Detroit 8v92Ti. She had three chairs, a mahogany transom and she was ready to go. She was beautiful and by October

1980, she was mine. I called her Best Revenge from the old proverb...living well is the best revenge.

Slips at the Fishing Center had to be earned and approved by the Board of Directors—a group composed of eight charter Captains. The first year we fished out of the Pirates Cove Marina. At the time Pirates Cove was fairly new, though it added an extra ten miles each way to the bridge to get out.

My captain was Charles, the younger brother of a captain who still runs his charter daily out of the Fishing Center. In year two, we were approved for a slip at the Fishing Center. Charles took a job on land and we were lucky enough to hire a new captain, a young Bull Tolson.

Tolson was fresh out of the cockpit of Tony Tillett's famed *Carolinian* (Tony is the younger brother of Omie Tillett!). Bull has gone on to become one of the most highly respected captains on the East Coast. Running the *Sea Toy* for many years, Tolson has won piles of tournaments on the East Coast and Bermuda. Recognized as one of the best, he's still hard at it in 2020...

We moved from Pirates Cove to the Fishing Center in the spring of 1982. Bull was a new captain then and the prevailing afternoon breeze was a strong and steady SSW coming straight up the creek. It ran crosswise to our slip. As we were getting rigged early one weekend, Bull was at the helm practicing docking his new ride.

Like most (read *all*) of the OI Captains, the trick to docking here was to understand the winds and tide before getting the boat set up. Once in position you had to throw her into reverse, back down (HARD...maybe even causing a wave coming over the transom!), get within a few feet of the concrete bulkhead, throw her into forward and bring her to dead stop.

This process would culminate with the boat being located so the mate could just drop the dock lines over the piling perfectly! Watching this get done was a thing of beauty. It was something only to be performed by an expert captain—a maneuver that required both confidence and experience. As I watched its performance from the dock—truth be told, I was just a bit terrified about what could become of my prized possession should something go wrong.

After watching this process expertly wielded three or four times, I had to ask the question... So I did. "Bull, I am hugely impressed by your boat handling skills, but what would happen if the throttle cable breaks when you throw her into forward?"

In response, my new young local Captain looked at me for a full two minutes before answering the question. In the most perfect Elizabethan dialect of Dare County, Bull said, and I quote directly, "Jay-eff, don't worry yourself. These things ain't nuthin but f'ing wood and glue. I'll jus glue the bitch back together and you'll never know!"

A more perfect answer simply does not exist!

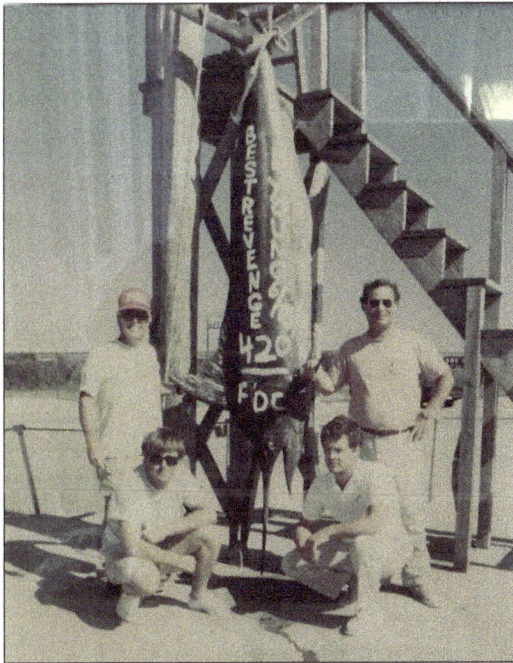

Photo taken possibly in 1982
Pictured left to right: Angler Dan Young (standing), Mate Charlie Dunn, Capt. Bull Tolson, and the author (also standing)

Boss Man,
Think Maybe I Could Get
a Little Advance?

Dare County in the early 70s was a wonderful place. It is a place secluded-- sheltered by the sea to the East, marsh and Sound to the West, barrier island to the South. From the North, a one lane road crossing the Pamlico Sound Bridge provided a single point of access... Dare County was, in many ways, its own world indeed.

Many of the Captains here and most all of the young Turks coming up as mates had never been out of the County! After all, there was really no need to leave. You had world class fishing all spring and summer and into the fall; world class deer and black bear hunting all winter. There were also jobs for anyone who wanted to work. Jobs in boat building, commercial fishing, recreational fishing — and of course captain and mate jobs.

As good as Dare County was, at the time it was truly insulated from much of the world. Mores existed for sure, but perhaps not the same as elsewhere. By the mid-80s I had another captain who joined the team in the late fall one year. At that time of year, there is generally not really much boat work to do. His job description basically involved boat upkeep and maintenance to get ready for spring fishing season. He was on the payroll on an hourly basis though, while he had another job with a local builder.

Late that December, I got the weekly status call. Toward the end of the conversation, the new captain asks, "Maybe I could get a $500 advance on the season?"

A bit taken by surprise, I answered that we could probably do so, before asking if everything was ok.

His answer was direct, "My wife is pregnant and due in January."

This response surprised me since we had discussed earlier that his wife had 100% insurance coverage in her job. Concerned, I asked if insurance had become a problem.

"Well, not really, her insurance will cover it all," he began. "But my girlfriend is also pregnant. She is due in February...and she has no insurance at all!"

I sent him the check that day.

Months later, while fishing together and sitting in the bridge, I mentioned the conversation about his "dilemma" and asked if all was ok. With a big smile, he answered, "Yep, no problem. All fine."

Upon hearing this response, I couldn't help but ask if there was any bad blood. Did wife and girlfriend know about the other? With another big smile, the captain answered, "Everybody's happy. Sure they know each other. They're good friends!"

I must have looked puzzled because he then added, "Hey, Boss Man, don't forget. This is Dare County, ain't it?"

Another correct, simple and perfectly logical answer.

CL Webster
and the Bucket List Fish

I got out of the Army in September of 1970. Most of my time in the service was dedicated to teaching scuba diving down near the Cambodian border. Thanks to my assignment, most of my time spent was on and in the ocean.

The ocean was my love, but, like everyone else, I needed a job. I needed a real job that paid real money. I was fortunate enough to be able to return to my pre Army job as a salesperson for Xerox Corp. I started back at Xerox two days after getting back from the Army!

I worked hard and I did well in the job, but I lived the sea, boats and fishing. One of my new buddies had a new, big (to me) fishing boat on the Chesapeake Bay. The boat was a 23' Formula. I loved it and fished with him every chance we found. We chased bluefish, stripers and sea trout. It was wonderful.

One day my then boss invited me to fish a two day charter out of North Carolina. Day one would take place in Hatteras and the second day in Oregon Inlet. The first day, fishing out of Hatteras on the *Stormy Duchess* with Emory Dillon as Captain and Chip Schafer as mate, we caught dolphin, a wahoo and then...the first blue marlin that I had ever seen! On the second day on the *Mel O Dee* with Captain Buddy Cannady and mate Billy McAskill out of Oregon Inlet, it was dolphin and two white marlin. I was done for-- I found heaven!

Over the next five years, I worked hard and spent every hour and every nickel on boats and fishing. In the boat department, I started with an old 18', then a newer 19, then a 25' Marauder, before opting for a new 23' Formula.

From there, I decided to buy the real thing and planned to purchase a 31' Bertram. Soon thereafter I saw the newly introduced Ray Hunt designed Tournament Fisherman by Chris Craft. I was intrigued by the boat. It managed to overcome many of the 31's problems. In terms of bridge size and cabin comfort the boat appealed to me. It also had a full beam and a drier ride. You guessed it, I bought the TF instead. For the record, I bought the boat new in Pompano Beach for $24,700 delivered. After outriggers, electronics (two radios, handheld RDF and paper based bottom machine) and used Rockaway chair, total invested...under $30K!

In the spring of 1975, I ran the boat from Florida up to Oregon Inlet. I began to fish offshore every weekend, often taking guys from work. A frequent offshore companion was my then boss, Bob Webster. Bob and I had worked together for the past year.

After one trip, Bob came to me with a personal request. "Would it be ok to bring my Dad offshore one weekend?" he asked. When your Boss asks a favor—especially one of such personal significance—you really have no option. So, next trip, here comes Dad.

Dad (CL Webster) was very tall, thin—nearly to the point of being gaunt, and clearly not in the greatest of health. A true gentleman, by the time of our trip CL was in his late 70s. He'd fished the Bay for his entire life. Not only that, he made his own bucktails and wrapped his own rod guides.

Soon after our introduction, he pulls me aside to tell me that he really wants to catch a marlin, a *blue* marlin no less, before he dies. He asked if I could help. Just a bit of pressure!

Off we head at daybreak the next day. On the boat were Bob and his Dad, two other work buddies and myself at the helm. We left late after it took CL a bit more time than expected to get ready.

It was a pretty day with winds light and variable. The seas were in the 2-3 feet range and crossing the bar was easy (which, in Oregon Inlet is not always the case). We didn't have far to go to reach The Point and we planned to put the lines out from there.

About five miles short of the Point, in forty fathoms of water, we hit a fully formed weed line. Looking around, we were all by ourselves. We stopped and decided to bail dolphin for a starter. Using dink rods, we get maybe a half dozen gaffers in the boat. Then it happens...

Sitting in a pile of dolphin, we are picking through them. We hook a peanut and are in the process of getting him to the boat. Out of nowhere a blue marlin swims up and eats it on the run! It was not a giant—but it was a *blue* marlin and CL had yet to die. We were onto something!

Quickly we get everything else in the boat. I'm holding the rod, which is now hooked to the blue marlin. Before I can get CL into the chair and hand him the rod, Bob pulls me aside. He's both excited and nervous. He tells me that he's worried that his Dad may have a heart attack.

My response is immediate... "And, if he does, is there a better way for him to go?"

Bob agrees. We put his Dad in the chair and put a harness on him.

The old man proceeds to fight his blue marlin for an hour and thirty minutes--- flawlessly! He couldn't have done it better if he were a 30 year old first class big game fisherman. He was great!

We took the fish (picture below) and made the old man proud. While this life long, 70-plus year old fisherman may have been proud in every way... he was not as proud as the rest of us were for him!

One of the finest moments of my life fishing was the look on that man's face when we boated his fish.

It weighed 225 pounds, but it might as well have weighed 2,000. We donated it to a local church. It doesn't get any better!

Author and CL Webster ... the bucket list fish!

Perspective

Ahh, perspective ... In the early 70's, my offshore exploits were centered around taking a week or two off during the summer and trailering my 23' Formula 233F from Virginia to North Carolina. Our tackle set up consisted of Penn Senator 114Hs, one borrowed 10/0 reel and a local freelance mate. The mate was there to rig baits, tell us where the Fleet was heading, and keep us out of trouble.

The mate was really there to help us catch fish. Were we to truthfully look back and analyze our situation, while we may have had limited information... we had even less skill! All that said, we were enthusiastic!

Our first year, 1971, was really a learning year. We did ok (barely). Not only did we have much to learn and figure out about fishing, we also had to figure out how (and who) to hire as a mate. Our last few days that year were with a new young guy, Snoopy. Snoopy really knew what he was doing and how to help us learn the game. The next year, we hired him for the whole two weeks of our fishing season.

In 1972, we did great! We learned tons and caught fish every day...tuna, mahi, wahoo, white marlin... On the next to last day, we found whites balling bait. Snoopy taught us what to do...and we caught and released 14 whites!

We had it figured out. It didn't matter that Snoopy was generally hungover each morning. Nor did it matter that he was inebriated once or twice at 5:00am when we met him...he'd sleep it off during slow times. He was our guy.

In 1973, Snoopy was still our guy. We booked him again for our two weeks straight. But, first day, 5:00am, no Snoopy!

Just minutes before we began to panic, a heavy set young guy came looking for us. He informed us that he was to be our mate. As it turned out, Snoopy was no longer coming to the marina because (drum roll, please) people there drank alcohol and smoked tobacco and chased women.

I guess we looked sorta surprised, so he explained further. Snoopy, he said, "Done found the Lord" and was now commercial shrimp netting in the Sound. Surprised, but glad to have a mate, we had a good two weeks again catching lots of fish and learning from the new guy. Everything went so well, in fact, that we booked him for the next year's two weeks!

When day one of our two week 1974 season rolled around, we headed to the marina to meet the new guy. Imagine our surprise when see there waiting to meet us were the new guy AND Snoopy—the latter of whom was clearly intoxicated, quite loud and very happy! He was going to be our mate for the two weeks.

This was good news, after all we had quite a history with Snoopy, but I was puzzled. I pulled new guy aside and asked, "I thought he done found the Lord?"

New guy looked me in the eye, and without cracking so much as a smile, said "Yep, that he did. But, the Lord wouldn't have him!"

Ahhh, perspective.... And for more perspective on those who frequented the marina and "drank alcohol and smoked tobacco and chased women," there is the following.

Given that the life of a mate consisted of long hours of difficult work, many had a hard time meeting girls. These difficulties became even more acute given that, because the mates had so little free time to invest, their interests were often rather "short term" shall we say. Given the time crunch—and the competition-- guys would often resort to finding ways to get noticed quickly. Two such approaches come to mind. While they may have a similar starting point, each takes on a slightly different spin.

The first guy would quickly size up the bar, decide who to approach, introduce himself and offer to buy a drink. This gesture was usually accepted. Then, upon learning her name, he would sit back and say quietly, "I just love your name, I have it tattooed on my body."

At that point, the conversation would generally become animated. If things went according to plan, they would have another drink or two...and he'd offer to show her his tattoo. Often enough, she would agree.

They would next head to his apartment or boat or car...at which time down came his pants and underwear. Then, sure enough, there, perfectly tattooed on his right cheek was "Your Name."

The second approach was similar, though it was more of a shotgun blast than a rifle shot. Our guy would be in the bar, start drinking and quickly become inebriated. Then, attracting as much female attention as possible, he would loudly brag about the fact that, even though most of the local boats were single engine, his was "twin screw." He'd then offer to prove it to anyone who wanted to know.

Things would then generally progress rather quickly. Often he would then find himself standing on a chair (or once or twice the bar) where he would drop his pants...And there on either cheek were propeller tattoos-- counter rotating no less! With this for starters, often enough our guy would find himself a willing participant for his night's activities!

Shotgun or rifle, each approach seemed to work.

Just bit more perspective....

SHARKS

It was the summer of 1976 and I had my 30'TF in its slip at the Oregon Inlet Fishing Center for the season. I was working for the Xerox Corporation as a Sales Manager in the Richmond Branch office. It was only three hours to the boat and fishing. Things were good. I was learning, picking up skills and tackle, and generally beginning to understand the ebb and flow of the when to fish where; what to use for different species.

Most fishing days were spent either working weed lines for mahi or current edges for yellowfin. Every now and again the occasional billfish would show...generally whites, a few sails and even a spearfish once in a while. The prize, of course, was a blue marlin... always the apex species.

In those days, we killed most billfish. Upon boating the fish, they brought to the dock and hung for pictures. After the photography sessions, the billfish were donated to one or more of the inland, generally poorer churches where they were distributed to the congregation for food.

At the time, in the mid-70s, this approach made sense. It would take years to understand stewardship of the species and that a release was just as impressive...even more so, really. (Note: the limit of 60 mahi per day had just been accepted by the Fleet-- the limit of three tuna per angler had not yet begun. It was "back in the day" for sure.)

July 20th was my birthday. For the day we planned the trip to be a five person crew. For whatever reason, two folks couldn't make it so we went off at daybreak with a crew of three. Aboard were myself, the mate and my buddy Kerry as the angler. The day started well with a handful of gaffers and two football sized yellowfin.

The seas calm. The water temperatures were warm and pilot whales were all around. Given the conditions, we decided to head "overboard" for marlin. We put out bigger baits with a blue/white Hawaiian Eye (now called an Islander) over a horse ballyhoo in right long rigger.

The fishing was slow. We trolled over the edge to the deep, then back in to the edge then back out to the deep. Not much was happening. Then just after midday, the right long popped and he was on!

It was a blue one. The fish was not huge but big, maybe 400--surely close. He was on a "50" spooled with 60-pound Ande mono. The fish spent the first half hour on the surface...greyhounding, then tailwalking and thrashing. After putting on a show up top, it sounded.

He fought long and hard. After maybe two hours, the oxygen debt built up and we had him. In the smooth seas we got him to the boat and hit him with the flyer. We got him cleated off easily.

By then boats had no gin poles for lifting and most didn't have "tuna doors." Generally, there would be enough crew to use wave action to lift the fish over a gunwale-- turn the broadside and use the lift then dip of the waves. We, however, had only three head and there was no wave action to help.

As we considered our (limited) options, it became apparent that we were running out of time-- quickly. One or two sharks (bulls I believe) had been around, but the flyer created a heavy blood trail. With a nice marlin bleeding and cleated off to the boat they came in droves.

One after the other tore into our fish that was laid up beside the boat. Taking big chunks with each bite, tearing 20 or more pounds of flesh with every sawing, ripping bite, it was carnage. It was over in less than 10 minutes. The water beside us was a bloody froth. The bill, head, gills and most of the backbone were left...nothing more.

This was my first experience with being truly unprepared; with not having a plan, with not knowing what to do. I learned.... It would not happen again!

The Development
of a Bottom Fishery
and Daytime Swordfishing

Throughout the 1970's as we caught our tuna, our blue and white marlin, along with the hands fulls of wahoo and sails thrown in for good measure, we often thought about what might be down deep on the bottom-- just waiting to be caught. The entire drop off from, say, the Hatteras Tower up to the Triple 0's just south of Virginia Beach had depth, structure, wrecks...It was a perfect combination.

It was clear that the area would hold fish of some kind or other, but the tackle and technology of the day made it pretty much out of reach. Stiff rods with International 80s—spooled with mostly Ande mono just would not work for deep water, bottom fishing applications.

Not only that, but depth finders were primitive compared to what is available today. Braided line had not yet been introduced. The reels of the day were not high gear ratio (one to one cranking makes for a lot of winding). Circle hooks had not arrived yet from Japan...Fishing the bottom structure in any meaningful way was just not in the cards at the time. This was not to mention the lack of accuracy of then NOAA charts—but at the time, how could you have known that they were inaccurate?

Fast forward to the time around 2010. By this time, technology had caught up with our curiosity about the benthos. Sportfishing was now equipped with high speed reels, braided line, bottom machines that reached the depths...and CHIRPed...it all fit together. Electric assist reels at reasonable prices finished the picture! Equipped with this wonderful new tool box, we began to explore and to learn.

What fish lived in the deep and where did they live? Did these bottom dwellers prefer structure or mud bottom? Was steep or flat bottom the prime real estate...for what fish and when?

Deep dropping as we now know it came to the East Coast around 2010. It is now firmly established within the repertoire for offshore trips. Still, for most guys, most trips are trolling...working the edges, the temp breaks, searching for birds and weed lines. Most trips fill the box to one degree or another. With the added wrinkle of deep dropping, sometimes we can pull victory from defeat. This adds a whole new "depth" to the offshore fishing experience. It also produces some of the best table fare around.

When fishing my boat offshore, the plan most days is to run to the edge and troll for the better part of the day. We then rig our deep drop outfit and give it a go. On most days, once we have found good sets of numbers, we can easily add a few tilefish to the box. Our tilefish are generally bluelines or goldens, depending on depth of drop... Goldens prefer mud bottom in 600 feet or more, bluelines like more structure and less depth.

Often we get rosebellies and occasionally a barrel fish or wreck fish. If we're fishing the Washington Canyon or South, we can pick up a snowy grouper too. And now and then (not good luck!) a warsaw grouper may well pick off your 30ish pound trophy and head for parts unknown. If it's not a big warsaw, it may well be some other sea monster that gobbles up your dinner! It's just part of it.

Sometimes, however trips are dedicated to pursuit of the resident masters of the deep. One such trip took place on September 12, 2019. We had planned a daytime trip for swordfish out of Oregon Inlet on the *Qualifier*. Captain Fin Gaddy and mate Colin Oxnard have the daytime swords dialed in. Years of learning and refining—where to fish, dialing in on the best baits and best tackle-- have brought them to the top of the pack when it comes to swordfishing teams north of the Florida Keys.

After hearing all about it for years, we decided to give it a shot. The first date we booked was in mid-August. It was a blow out, but when Fin called and said that September 12 looked good. We took it.

The team was my longtime friend (and daughter's godfather) Joe Perez and Dave Mutzabaugh. Dave and I had been friends and worked together since 2002. All of us were experienced offshore fishermen who wanted to learn and understand daytime swordfishing.

At 5:00am we left the dock. We ran 55 miles to a deep mud bank that Fin had successfully fished before. Our first drop was at 7:30 am. We were fishing a deep line and buoy line. The seas were calm and the weather perfect — maybe 75 degrees with soft sunlight. We were fishing in about 900 feet of water. Our deep bait was 100 feet off bottom.

We fished a long drift, both lines out. There was lots of life around us. Sharks wandered by, passed a dolphin patch as we drifted through scattered grass. There was even a free jumping blue marlin a few hundred yards out.

Then the deep rod dipped and loaded up, but no hookup. The bait, a rigged goggle eye, came up mangled and the leader was a bit scored, but no hookup. We dropped again and fished another hour. The deep rod dipped quickly twice. We moved the bait up about 50 feet and waited. There was no follow up bite. After another 10 minutes, we picked up to find another mangled bait, but again no hook up.

Fin decides to move. We run off another 12 miles East Northeast to our second spot. This one is of similar depth has a bit sharper drop off-- the contour lines are bit closer. We're fishing in about 1000 feet.

We dropped again, both lines. The conditions are still calm and perfect. We're drifting slowly, keeping the boat ready. Both lines are deployed off the stern, each is quartering starboard. All eyes are fixed on the rod tip and the buoy.

Then, boom, the buoy just disappeared in an instant. The rod is loaded up and line is screaming from the reel. The fight was mainly deep. The fish was making blistering short runs against 22 pounds of steady drag.

Soon the fish was up and down in the water column. We'd gain then lose, gain then lose. Over time we started to gain bit by bit. It was a strong fish that never jumped, just fought deep. After about an hour, there it was—color!

Our fish was not a sword. He was a bigeye thresher—a shark. It was a huge fish, well over 500 pounds. With its tail (for which the thresher is named) the beast was maybe 15-16 feet long. It was an absolutely beautiful animal. The fish had a huge deep body, eyes as big as saucers, and pectoral fins so wide that they looked like airplane wings. We released him.

With the shark released, we redeployed the two lines. Not 10 minutes go by when the deep rod goes off. The rod is fully loaded—a clean hookup on the strike. The fish gobbled up a rigged eel.

After the initial run, he came in easily. For parts of the fight, aside from a few headshakes, we weren't certain he was still on. There was no pull, no run, and generally not much resistance.

As we retrieved the line, we reached 150 feet—at which point sat the weight. It was connected to the line with a wax loop designed to be able to be removed by the mate at this point in the fight. We were fishing an RJ Boyle "medium" rod, loaded with 80-pound Spectra braided line. The leader was 150 feet of 200 pound mono with a bite leader of eight feet 300 pound. The rig was baited with goggle eye or squid or eel on heavy 12/0 hook. As he reaches for the lead, Colin says softly, "Sometimes there's no fight…until the weight comes off…"

Big Eye Thresher (about 500ish) — Released

Wow, was he ever correct! As soon as we took the weight off of the main line, the fish went completely wild. It started by jumping maybe 100 yards out. Then it immediately headed straight to bottom in less time than seemed possible. Then it came back up and jumped again...then back to the bottom.

And so it went, against 22-pounds of fixed drag for over an hour—with no sign of weakening. Then slowly, bit by bit, we gained a few turns here then a turn or two there. From 900 feet down to 750, then to 500 than ever so slowly, we had him turned. By about 2:10 we had color for the first time. We hooked the fish just before

1:00. Colin readied dart. By 2:20 the fish was in range and Colin hit him with the dart. It was a perfect shot. We had him.

Two of us held on with hand gaffs. Fin came down off the bridge and opened the tuna door. Maneuvering a fish attached to a four foot sword in such a way as to fit through a tuna door can be something of a challenge, but we got him turned and wrangled into the boat. The fish was lying on cockpit floor.

He was perfect, a beautiful fish. Guesses of weight ranged from 300-350. It measured some 88" from the tip of the lower jaw to fork of its tail.

I, for one, was in awe of this fish. I'd caught a few in the past and seen five caught in one day riding out with Nick Stanzcyk (100-150 ish) but this one was different, at least to me. From its depth of color, to the jumps and the fight...everything about this fish was glorious. Now he was in the cockpit!

L to R: Capt. Fin Gaddy, the author, Joe Perez,
and Dave Mutzabaugh

After we got the fish situated, it was exactly 2:30-- time to head for the barn...happy. Fin comes down and we sit in the salon, relaxed, and contented all the way around. We talk about family, fishing, values, and life is good.

Back to the dock we take a couple pictures and then we weigh the fish. Fin called the weight to be about 325. The scale read 316. The fish probably would have been 325 when it first hit the deck.

The Fishing Center was not too crowded that day. Together we cut the fish up quickly. It was a pumpkin sword. Its flesh tinted orange, with touch of pink...glorious animal. Not all swordfish are pumpkins—catching one is a treat. They are prized by chefs, and old fishermen alike for their rich flavor. I took two chunks, maybe 25 pounds each, and drove straight home to Delaware. My wife had been sick and I wanted to get home.

The next night we grilled the first of our swordfish steaks. It was like butter. Served with squeeze of lime, a touch of butter sauce and mashed capers, it just does not get any better!

THE FIGHT N LADY:
A CAROLINA CLASSIC

In the early 70's the fleet at Oregon Inlet Fishing Center (OIFC) consisted of some 30 charter boats, almost all run by owner operators, almost all single engine, much like today. The newer boats were likely to be the 37'ers built by Warren O'Neill, pushed often by Cummins 903s running roughly 16-18 knots. The older rigs, like the *Jerry Jr.* and the *Erma Queen*, had the old style canoe stern, workboat lines and paddled along at maybe 14 knots...maybe.

Events of the spring of 1974 though caused a bit of a stir. *The Gal O Mine* built by Omie Tillett was splashed. She was built for Big Al, Allan Foreman, a local charter captain.

She was big... some 53'. And she was fast... 23 knots at 1850 turns being pushed by a Detroit 12v71 Ti. Even then she still had more in reserve. And she was beautiful-- a proud bow, lots of flare, sweeping sheer line, with gleaming Awl Grip to show her off! Some folks even commented that her size and power might just cause her to break up in heavy seas!

Well, not only did she not break up, she ushered in a new era. The following spring, Buddy Davis splashed his hull number one, the 46' *Capt BC* for Buddy Cannaday. Capt. Buddy who soon would follow and begin building boats himself! The *Capt BC* was pushed along at 21 knots powered by a single 8v71Ti.

But, the *Gal* was Queen of the Fleet. With Big Al at the helm, she'd leave daily at daybreak. She was the first out and the first back. She even had the then unheard of electronic marvel that was radar!

On more than one occasion in fog or heavy rains most others followed her.

By the early 80s, Big Al bought a strip of marshland on Roanoke Island and sold the *Gal* to Jap Richardson, likely who hired Benjie York as captain. At this time, the *Gal* was docked right beside my partner's 35' Harris, a private rig. We marveled often at how well the *Gal* rode and how comfortable she was; how many folks could relax in her huge cockpit.

Well, of course the inevitable took place. My partner, Capt. Joe Perez, bought the *Gal* from Jap in the early 80's! Joe hired the best. He hired Capt. Sam Stokes as full time captain and changed the boat's name to *Fight N Lady*.

Sam and Joe ran her through the 80s, amassing a record of successes along the way. The highlight of their partnership took occurred with a 1020 pound blue marlin in 1985. At the time, it was the third largest Atlantic blue ever taken in the world! Add in the countless limits of tuna and dolphin, the big eyes and the years of multiple releases of white marlin, theirs was an enviable record.

By the mid-90s the Detroit 12 was getting tired. It was wheezing a bit, smoking a bit, and generally in need of replacement. A new power plant was installed-- a 3412 Caterpillar, manual not electronic, that brought her up to 1050 horsepower. Now, her cruise increased to 25 knots and her fuel burn went down. A typical full day offshore run? 130-140 gallons. She was now efficient enough to make her profitable to run even with fluctuations in fuel pricing.

Through the 90s the *Lady* remained a top boat. In fact her tee shirts have been seen not only in the world's best fishing spots, but also in places like Bangkok, Copenhagen, Lucerne and on and on. Sam ran her generally with Joe filling in as needed.

As the times changed, Joe talked seriously about perhaps building a new *Lady*. The newer rigs were now pushing 60', cruising 25 knots plus and gorgeous to look at. But, every time he crunched the numbers and did the analysis, it was crystal clear…the *Fight N Lady* was the perfect combination. She was fully updated, beautiful to look at, still fast, economical and great in any sea!

Fast forward to 2018. Sam has retired, Joe still runs her on occasion. A new and capable captain, Roger Parker, is at the helm (he was the mate for many years before getting his ticket). She stays fully booked and continues as one of the top boats in the Fleet! In June 2018, I took a friend on her for a two day busman's holiday. We had a limit of tuna by 9:30am Wednesday and a limit of dolphin by 9:30 Thursday. The trip was capped off by a sailfish release, and we were back at the dock by 1:00! And her powerplant? Over 30,000 hours, running strong as new. Her oil is changed religiously and the risers every five years or so!

Just a side note: to give you an idea of the forward thinking of Big Al, her first owner and Captain, the piece of marshland that he bought in 1980? Today it's known as "Pirates Cove."

Originally published, Sep. 28, 2018 on InTheBite.com

"Jeff and I have been friends since the early 70s, we've owned boats and hunting property together. We've hunted and fished in some of the world's best places, but Oregon Inlet always remains at top of the list. We've had the good fortune to personally know some of the best Captains and boat builders in the industry. And, we still manage to fill the box…often with a compass, radio and bottom machine that occasionally works."

- **Captain Joe Perez**
Owner of *Fight n Lady*, Omie Tillett Hull #2,
Oregon Inlet

STRAFED!
HERE COME THE FEDS ...

It was December 2016 and we were trolling for striped bass off of the Delaware coastline. The fall striper migration reaches its peak from mid-November through December off the New Jersey, Delaware and Maryland coasts. In most years there are many fish in the run.

Most of the fish are large—the type clearly protected by strong State and Federal Laws. The presiding State law at this time was a one fish per person slot limit with fish from 37-44" protected (you could keep one fish per person per day, it had to be less than 37" or more than 44"). The Federal Law, however, strictly protects fish lying beyond the three mile limit that separates state jurisdiction from federal waters.

Given how the law works, the striper trolling fleet works up to, but not over the line. Coast Guard cutters work the line, so do small planes with cameras. Occasionally a helicopter comes by. Nobody intentionally works over the line. If you're photographed fishing on the wrong side of the line, you receive a summons to court and an extremely hefty fine. Even when schools of big cow stripers are breaking the surface, you just don't cross into Federal water.

One day that December we were out striper fishing, it was around noon. It was a calm day, with temperatures in the high 40s. The fish are scattered but present enough to keep the fleet busy working several lumps close to the edge. I am driving friend's boat, a fully rigged out 31' Contender.

The owner is a commercial airline pilot. In addition to his boat, he is part owner of a small plane, a Cessna 182RG. The fleet is crowded, but we have an 18" GPS screen and full electronics so, I don't mind working close to the line. We are fishing maybe 30 yards closer than other boats around us. We stay well aware of our exact location and even when hooked up we stay very inside the line, but we're close.

Sometime in the middle of the afternoon all of a sudden the radio chatter heats up and gets frantic! Then quickly approaching from the North is a small plane... It is heading directly for us and fast! It is flying maybe 50 yards off the water.

Just as it approaches, the plane seems to shake it wings. Just as it shakes, it drops a package of some sort dropped strategically close to us. The mystery package damn near hits us! The plane veers off, banks and comes back... It comes back again and again, then again, dropping several times...almost hitting us!

The radio chatter was deafening. The consensus over the airways was rock solid and universal. That blue Contender crossed the line and "they" dropped dye packets to mark it. "Boy, are they gonna get a fine...maybe they'll lose the boat! Those guys are in big, big trouble." And on and on and on. We said nothing, just maintained radio silence!

One week later, I was coming in from a morning deer hunt with bunch of buddies. We grabbed cups of coffee and recounted the day's hunt. Before long, the talk switched to fishing. The topic quickly became "the blue boat, the dye packets and wonder about what happened to them!"....

Finally, I couldn't hold back any longer. I let the cat outta the bag! "Boys, time to fess up," I said. "I was at the helm of the blue boat, we never crossed the line. The dye packets were actually bunches of bananas! The owner's buddies took his plane, loaded up 40 pounds of bananas and proceeded to bombard us!"

NEVER in the history of the Mid Atlantic have bananas been at the center of so much legal conjecture!

For the record, we did catch four keepers over 45" that day…. and one 50' Monster Bass.

THE JAPANESE SCRAPBOOK

It was midwinter in 1975. It was cold and damp in the Mid-At-lantic as most all midwinters are...but this winter we had a bonus planned. A group of us convened on a friend's 46' Bertram in St. Thomas in February for two weeks of fishing and running around the Islands. "Running around the islands" always seemed to include its share of drinking and raising Hell.

This was a private boat trip devoid of agendas or itineraries. We were intent on just fishing and fun...and had plans for lots of both. My job for the fishing was primarily as mate although we did switch around a bit.

We left Red Hook and crossed to the British side. We started out fishing the South Drop, working from Rams Head on St. John, all the way up the chain to Salt and Peter Island, trolling the drops and edges all the way.

We were fishing mostly rigged ballyhoo with sea witches on #12 wire....single strand. At the time this was pretty much all we knew. We were experiencing good fishing for white marlin, with occasional dolphin in the mix.

It was all good. The weather held, we caught plenty of fresh fish for our grill...and even got a free bottle of rum with every 100 gallons of fuel we bought. What's not to like?

At some point in the trip, a winter swell (the result of a heavy northeast wind) started to lay out, so we decided to give the North Drop a go. The North Drop would provide us a better shot for blue ones and generally more action all the way around. In addition to the fishing considerations, we could anchor overnight in Little Harbor and trade fresh dolphin or tuna for lobster dinners and drinks.

So, off we run...18 knots with 8v71ti's pushing the heavy 46' loaded with not only fuel but seven guys and a full complement of gear. We passed through the Tortola/Jost Van Dyke cut, passed Anegada and were off to the Drop.

Once there, the fishing alternated between good and great. We released two blues, several whites and had enough meat fish daily for dinner trade. Although it was rougher than hell (even as the swell subsided a bit), it was a glorious time for bunch of young guys.

As the trip progressed we settled into a bit of a daily routine. Sometime around midafternoon, we'd typically pack up the spread and head to the anchorage to wash down. From there, we'd scrub the boat and ourselves before heading for Sydney's Peace and Love... our nightly dining destination. Usually we'd bring a couple tuna or dolphin to be used in bartering for our dinner.

On our next to last day, we caught a large wahoo that changed our routine. If memory serves, the fish weighed 78 pounds. It was a good wahoo.

A couple of the guys suggested that we just have dinner on the boat. After all, they said, you really cannot beat fresh grilled wahoo steaks—especially if they are served with lots of rum. Their argument was sound and everyone soon agreed.

The boat needed fuel. I offered to clean and steak the 'hoo while boys fueled up and scrubbed the boat. We fueled on Tortola, but the boys dropped me off at Cane Garden Bay to clean and steak our wahoo.

Equipped with the fish, a cooler, and a sharp knife I disembark at Cane Garden Bay. There was really nowhere to easily clean a big fish, so I headed off a ways in search of a suitable location. I was wearing khaki shorts and flip flops. I didn't bring along any rags or have any towels handy. Looking down at my khaki shorts, I begin to think that this might be a bit more difficult than I imagined.

As I pondered my situation, a plan emerged. I was maybe a quarter mile from town along a sandy beach and it was by now late afternoon. There was not a soul to be seen. My plan was to take my shorts off (I had nothing under them of course), leave the flip flops on the beach, and walk out into knee deep water to steak the fish. This way, I figured, I wouldn't need any rags and didn't need to worry about getting my shorts bloody either. There was plenty of clean salt water—I'd just slice fish and pop steaks into the cooler... perfect.

As I was about halfway through dispatching the wahoo, things were going well. The knife was sharp, the cooler was half full, and I was standing in knee deep water with my back to the beach. I was in deep concentration.

Then, out of my reverie I hear a loud voice. The voice was clear and it spoke English with a heavy accent.... Jolted from my concentration, it occurs in my head that perhaps I have company.

Without thinking, I quickly turn around to see who is there. Turning around, and providing something like some might call a "full frontal", I come face to face with a tour bus...full of Japanese tourists!

The bus was full and it seemed like each tourist had a camera. Every passenger was by now happily snapping my picture. Were this sight not strange enough, the guide's voice come over the loudspeaker...."This is how the local island natives clean their fish!"

I sometimes think about that day on the beach. It makes me laugh. I also laugh when I think about the prospect of 50 year old naked pictures of me adorning vacation scrapbooks in Osaka or Tokyo. This may have been my earliest claim to marginal fame...?

The Greatest Fishing Story Never Told

(Sometimes, even about fishing...
your wife is correct!)

It was June, 2010. By this time, several conditions in my life conspired favorably for my fishing habit. Given that I had retired fairly young – at the age of 62, owned a fun boat that was good for all kinds of fishing and lived three miles from the marina, I began the habit of going to the marina every day.

On nice days (read calm seas here), I would head out to fish. Although I maintained no schedule really, my plans often involved heading out about 10:00am. I often times picked up a buddy or two at the marina or the tackle shop for company, but would not do so religiously.

Some context here will help....

1). I fish out of Indian River, Delaware. We have great fishing pretty much year round with summer fishing generally bottom fishing for flounder and sea bass. This fishery is located within maybe 10-15 miles from the Inlet and is generally structure-oriented--wrecks, rubble, coral beds and the like. On the whole, it is easy and fun.

2). My boat is fast. On most days, she has a 35 knot cruise, on calm days 40 knots. She carries a complete accompaniment of offshore equipment, full electronics and 300 gallons of fuel.

3). The Canyons that we fish—such as the Baltimore, Wilmington, and Poor Mans, etc-- are from 65-75 miles out. This might sound far, but on a calm day it's an easy run.

4). My wife has no interest in the boat nor in fishing. She has however, in matters such as these there is always a "but"), repeatedly "suggested" (read "forbid" here) that I do not go offshore alone... Bottom fishing solo is fine, but heading offshore is a no go...No!

So, with the above in mind, on the nicest days, we'd occasionally run to the deep. We'd usually start with a plan to stay inshore, but, sometimes, the pull of the deep would be too much and off we'd go.

Generally, I'd shove off the dock at 10:00 and be in 40 fathoms by 11:30. From there I'd put out the lines and work the radios to find the bite… if any were happening. Generally, one or two folks would join me, some just for company and some knew the game. We would fish for three or four hours, catch our share and get back in time for a cold one.

However, once in a while, the conditions would be perfect but no one would be around to come out and play. By now it should be no surprise to anyone reading this book, what might come over a red-blooded fisherman like myself in such a situation. I'd just saddle up and go offshore by myself. Yes, I know the risks for sure, but yep, I did it anyway.

Never to be accused of being foolish, I took precautions on days when I fished alone. I'd keep a portable waterproof VHF in my pocket, always wear my life preserver on and stay near the fleet. Rather than fish a set up that I couldn't manage, I would set out a simple spread.

My offshore solo fishing arsenal consisted of three 50W's-- two on long riggers and one shotgun. I placed them all in rod holders that I could reach from the helm and rigged them all with single dead baits attached to Islanders or Joe Shutes. This approach worked really well and I caught a lot of fish on the troll. On the few times that I did venture offshore by myself, I would finish my day with one drop for tilefish and then head for the barn. It felt good to fish like this-- always in radio contact, never out of sight of the fleet...bad habit indeed.

One day in early June, all of the conditions came together perfectly—save for one. It was a flat calm day and the fishing had been good offshore, I just couldn't find a companion. Overcome by the urge, I set out alone.

I deployed my three rod spread. The water was indigo blue over the edge. There were whales, there were birds, and there was bait... It was perfect.

All of a sudden, with no expectation, all three rods went off at once! It was as if each of the baits had been dropped into a speeding locomotive. In minutes the port rigger reel was dumped—the line gone.

I grabbed the starboard rod, spun the boat, picked up a bit of line. From there, I turned on the autopilot and began to consider my options. I was engaged in hand to hand combat, all by myself (outnumbered but not afraid!) with what was clearly a wolf pack of Big Eyes. Not to mention that the fish bit at mid-day in bright sunshine, but this never would have happened had I brought along a guest!

Doing battle with multiple sea monsters that are ensnared at the same time is an exercise that requires strategy—a strategy that is not too different from the triage approach used by emergency room doctors. Even when equipped with multiple anglers and multiple deckhands, captains will generally focus on getting one fish in a time. This is sometimes luck of the draw, but most of the time the approach involves choosing whatever fish is closest and focusing on that fish first.

I ignored the shotgun center rod, focusing all of my attention on the one fish. After an hour and a half of give and take, I got him close enough to hit with the flyer. After sticking, I got him cleated off and then, with much difficulty, managed to get him over the transom, through the door and into the cockpit.

This fish by itself would have been a trip maker. I was as exhausted as the fish. After getting him situated, I sat down on the bloody, wet deck and just rested. I may have even closed my eyes for a few seconds. Then I noticed the center rod.

Thankfully (or not thankfully) there was still line on the reel. The spool was maybe half gone and the rod was slightly bent as if pulling grass...Slowly, I got myself together to bring it in.

As soon as I touched the reel, the rod bent sharply and line began screaming off the reel! The second member of the wolf pack of bigeyes was still connected and had apparently been gently following the boat for maybe two hours by this point...Here we go again.

You guessed it. Another hour and twenty minutes and another strike with the flying gaff were followed by figuring out how to get another monster tuna into the boat by myself. After 15 minutes of wrangling boat side—"heaving and hoing" in every way I could think of, I had two medium sized bigeyes in the boat.

Now totally whipped—at this point I was more beat than the fish, I was outnumbered in the cockpit, two to one. Now I did fall asleep on the deck with a bigeye on each side of me... with the autopilot on, idling toward home. Old guys get tired more quickly than they admit.

After a good half hour, I got my second or *third* wind and took the helm. I picked up our speed and headed home. Upon getting to the dock, the bigeyes weighed in at 156 and 158 pounds.

I was pleased with my catch...BUT (there's that "but" again) I faced great peril were this story to make its way back to my wife. Were I to have relayed the story as it happened, divorce court could well have awaited in the future. I couldn't say this one or that one was with me! What to do?

Well, given the risks of the story, until this writing, I had only shared this story twice...and most certainly with folks way far away from my stomping grounds. And, truth be told, I have not gone to the deep alone since. The two fish whipped me good and I learned that it's not only weather and mechanical breakdown that you must contend with while offshore. Sometimes things come together too well.

I couldn't tell the story the day that it happened. And by the time I arrived at the dock with the bigeyes, the fleet had left for home...and it was a lonely ride to the barn. They say "Hell hath no fury like a woman scorned..." but this is to say nothing of what may result from violating the rules expressed in care and concern by a woman who knows you well enough to try to protect you from the call (and potential peril) of fishing offshore alone. Until now, the tale of the lone old guy against three 150-plus pound bigeye was perhaps my greatest fishing story never told.

**Fruit of
the Forbidden Tree!**

PHOTOGRAPHS

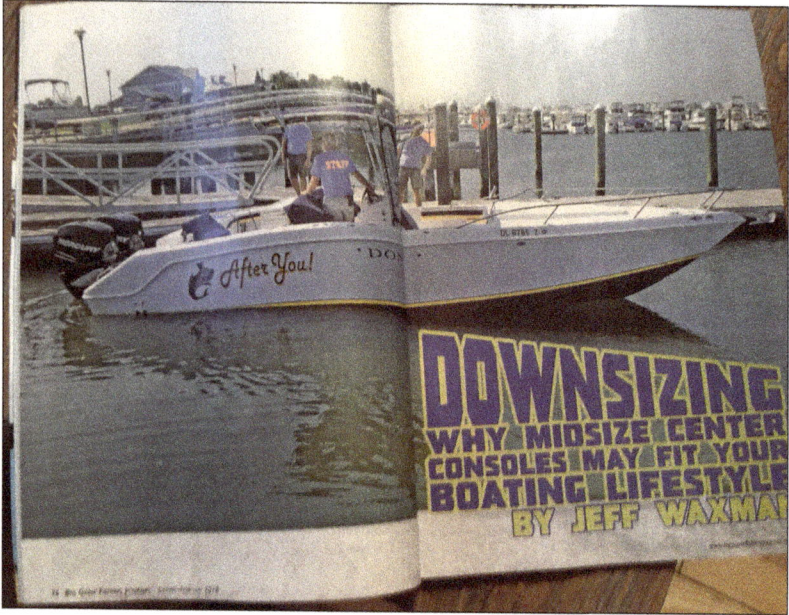

Article in *Big Game Journal* in 2015
on trend towards center consoles

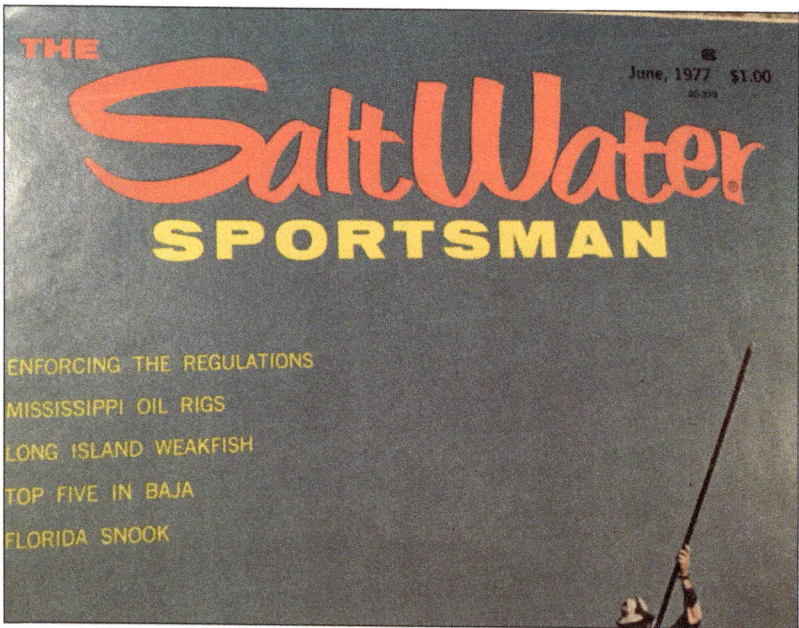

First article published in 1977 — *Salt Water Sportsman*
Note the price!

Stripers 46-49"
Released nine others that trip in December 2014

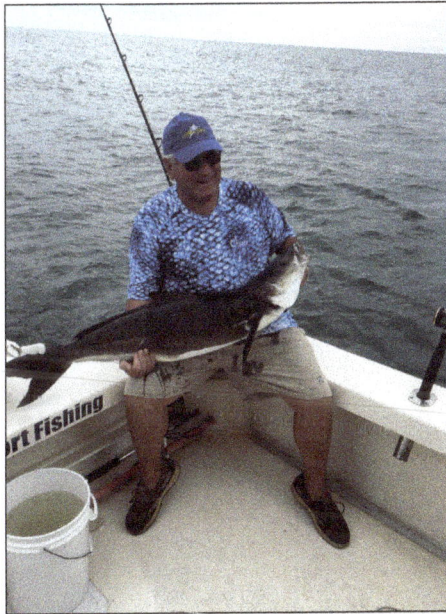

Author with Cobia CBBT
Caught 18 that day to 55lbs.

Blueline Tile

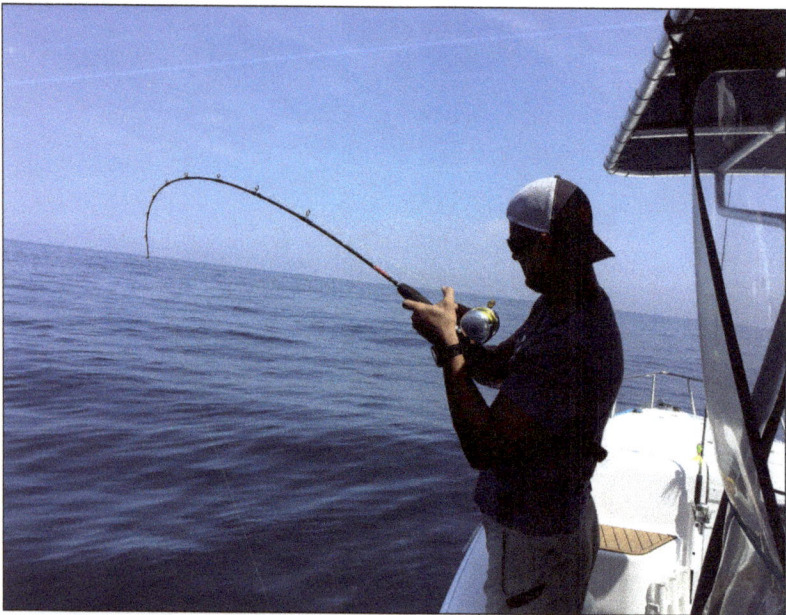

Dr. Jason Yonker - deep jig hookup in 700 feet depth

Blueline Tile — missed record by one ounce!

Golden Tile

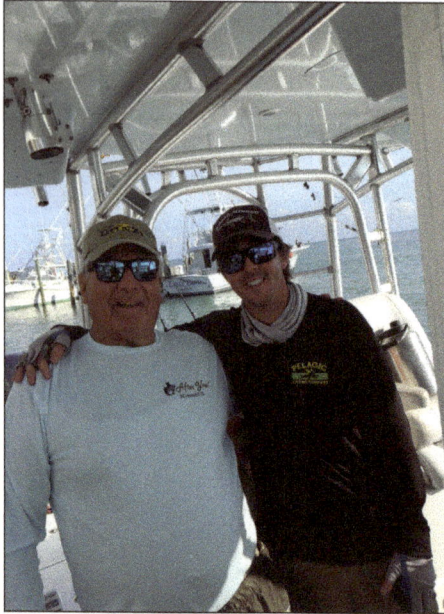

Author and Nick Stanczyk
Five swords released by 2:30

Sword (316 lbs)

Chris TF in Walker's Cay, 1976
Bikini soft top and Penn senators

Sashimi — fresh!

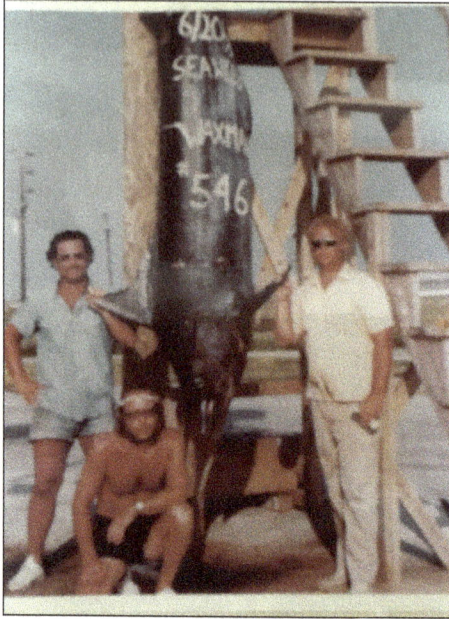

Blue One (546 lbs), 1975 - author standing on left
Few days after losing huge blue after nine hour fight!

TF running

Marauder - West Coast rig
Weird boat indeed!

Formula 233 - rigged! - in 1972

Best Revenge, 1981

Pomfret

Sword release

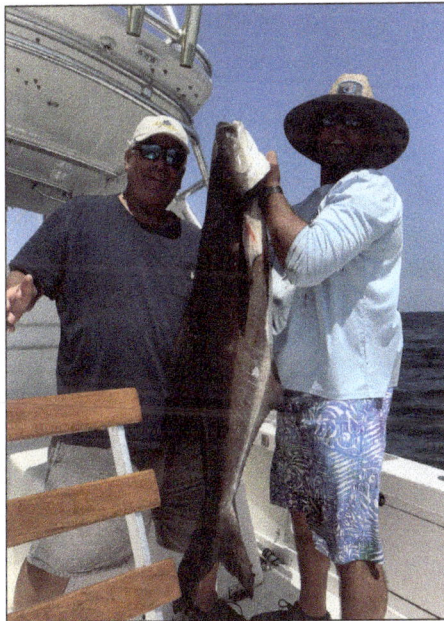

Cobia (45 lbs or so)
with Steve of Winking Blue Marlin Fame

Author and white one on *Sea Flame*
Still at it!

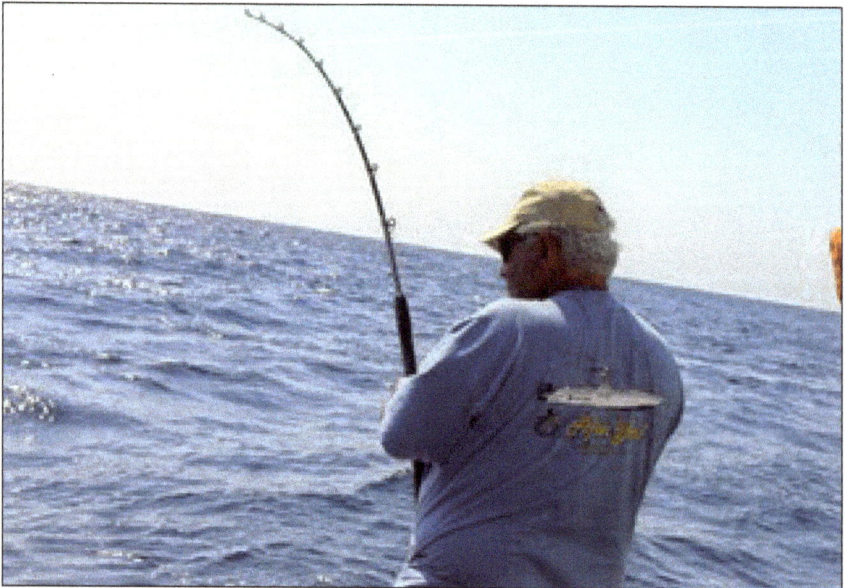

Author on billfish
(Old guy still having fun!)

Cobia, off the beach in Delaware
Largest at 45 lbs

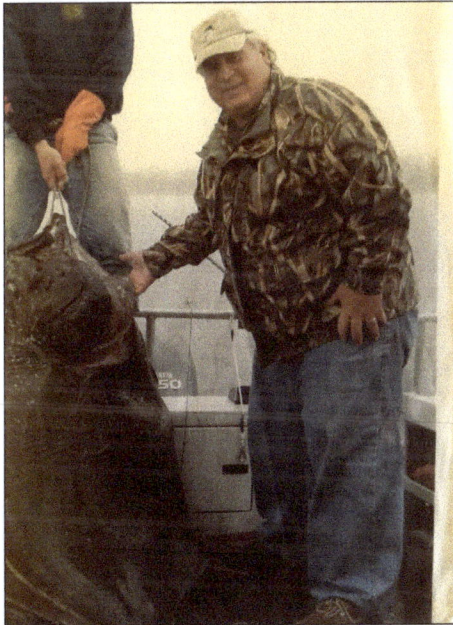

Quick trip to Alaska
Halibut (244 lbs) — Helluva Flounder!

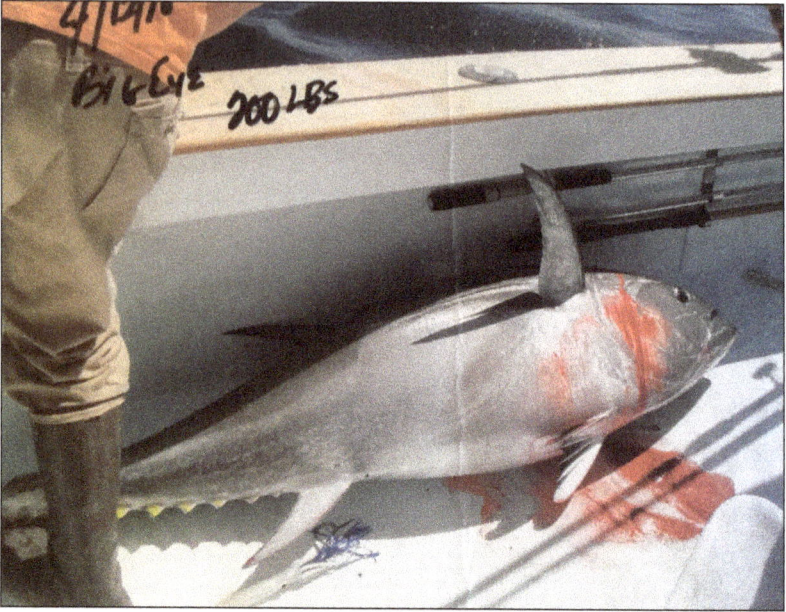

Tuna

More Tuna!

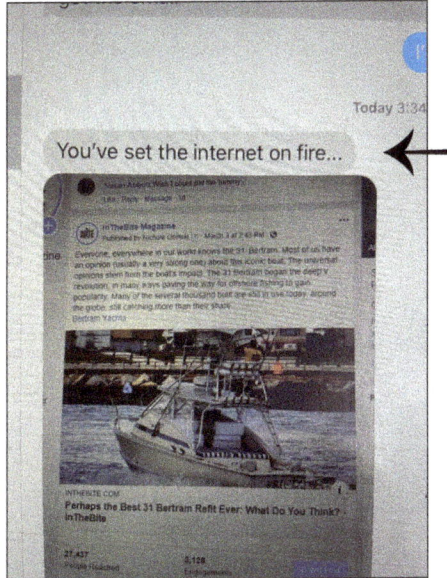

Author's article from Oct 2019 on *Priceless*, 31' Bertram owned by Dr. Pat Petrera with note from *In The Bite* magazine after it went on the Internet - 31s are popular!

Back in the day at OIFC: Capt. Mike Merritt, Charlie Kratz standing left, author kneeling left, mate (Bobby Croswaite?) kneeling, Tom Carey standing right in 1976

Thresher

Sheepshead (12 lbs)

Author and happy mate, Rodney Evans
49" Striper (45 lbs)

Good blueline catch: several 20 lbs plus

Typical catch in the Keys: yellowtails, cobia, snappers, king mackerel, etc.
Couple of hours on the reef!

Current boat: mid-size center console.
Out and back quickly; wash down in fifteen minutes.

My Fishing and Hunting buddy, my daughter, Jessi
Here she is with Marvin, her pet moose!
(She's standing on her deck.)

Section 2:

Lessons from Boats and Fishing

FOOLS AND LITTLE CHILDREN

It was the summer of 1960 and I was turning 14 years old. With the proceeds from two summers mowing lawns and two winters shoveling snow, I bought my first BIG boat! I found her by the roadside in a central New Jersey town with a "For Sale" sign. For $300 she was mine!

As the new owner of a 1954 Trojan Sea Queen, I was in heaven. She was a 14'6" plywood hulled beauty-- complete with a Mercury Mark 20 (pull start) outboard that was rated at all of 18 horsepower! To my eye, she was beautiful indeed. Now, I was ready to head off-shore and do battle with fluke and bluefish...like the big guys!

As it turned out, my inability to drive caused a minor problem. My folks contributed $40 to the cause and the next thing you know I had a slip at Great Kills Marina on Staten Island. With my sleeping back packed, I spent many nights that summer tucked under the little cabin (well, half of me tucked under the cabin).

I earned food and gas money by cleaning fish that came in on headboats and charters. The going rate was 10 cents a pound! I filled my 10 gallon gas can often and fished the Raritan Bay. I learned how to catch pretty well.

As good as all of this was, there was something missing. The charter guys came in with big bluefish daily. Sometimes they brought in a few bonito and even a tuna or two. Knowing where to go and what to do was the question.

That summer my boat's navigation system consisted of a Texaco gas station map. Somehow it turned out to not be of much help. Soon a plan emerged! I'd follow the charter boats out, watch what they do and catch big fish. After all with my two Penn 60s on stiff boat rods, I was ready.

Follow them out I did! The only problem was that they went far further than expected. Looking at my tank, I soon realized that more than half of my fuel was used! Finally, they stopped and started fishing. The fishing is a separate story for another time (it was better than hoped) but suffice to say that, given the predicament, I needed another plan.

My plan emerged. I would leave fishing early, head back a bit and when a boat came by, I would ask for a tow back in. All I had to do was leave enough fuel to get from where they dropped me off at the slip to fill the gas can.

My plan worked! It worked flawlessly. It worked so well, in fact, that after a few days of contemplation...I did it again! I caught more big fish—the same results! The plan worked...again and even again, it kept working! I was in the big leagues...

But, like all poorly conceived plans, it came to a crashing halt. After maybe three weeks and half dozen or more trips, I waved my canoe paddle and a familiar looking boat came to get me. The captain leaned over and asked, "Didn't I tow you in just last week?" I was so busted and embarrassed.

Later that day, a very nice and understanding charter boat captain came and found me on my boat. He sat down on the dock and gently explained to a sheepish and embarrassed young man about the vagaries of weather and currents and things like radios. It has turned out to be maybe the best lesson I ever received.

After patiently explaining all of this to me, the Captain shook my hand and told me to come find him in a year or two and maybe I could work as a mate on his boat! A year later...My first real paying job was as a mate on *The Chief.*

Thanks Captain. Thanks for understanding how a young guy thinks (and for maybe even saving my life!)

The Bucket

My best friend kept a charter boat at Oregon Inlet for years (see story on *Fight N Lady*). The boat was Omie Tillett's hull #3, a 53 footer. Powered by single 3412 Cat, she had a 23-24 knot cruise.

The boat featured a large salon complete with club chairs, a full sofa and assorted end tables, etc. Built for the local sea conditions, she was generally a very comfortable ride indeed. Once or twice a year, my buddy would set up a fun trip with a bunch of friends on a "busman's holiday."

Over the years, as is perhaps natural, I found myself liking rough seas less and less. This aversion was partly due to tougher fishing conditions, but more the result of my starting to get seasick. While I'd never get sick on a gas boat, the smell of diesel combined with a predawn start would make me queasy. If the seas were stacked up high and at close interval, sea sick I'd become.

Sure enough on the day of this particular busman's holiday, as soon as we crossed the bar I knew it was coming! Our group consisted of me and five friends. The seas were running six feet plus, with a very short interval. Beyond the short and choppy sixes there were the occasional 8-10 footers in the mix.

There are many ways to describe days like this... Some would say "sporty," I would say "nautical." The prevailing winds coupled with our condition mitigated speed of roughly 15-16 knots and caused the worst "station wagon effect" (wherein the winds and speeds combine to create a vacuum sucking the exhaust fumes straight into cockpit and salon)I can remember. A half hour into the run I grabbed a bucket.

We trolled for the next six hours—with riggers up to be safe (so the waves didn't snap them off). I have no idea what we caught, although once or twice I think we slowed down and voices got loud and I may have even heard a tail smack or two on the deck. Truth be told, I spent that entire trip lying on the salon floor curled up around and hugging my bucket.

Not only was I hugging it, I was often hurling into the bucket—they were dry heaves by midday. While some sleep came in and out, I mostly just lay there. Given that my buddies had driven five hours the night before to fish, I had to stick it out.

At about 2:30, we headed for the barn. It was still rough and the seas were still miserable and confused seas. We should not have been out there. But, we were… and now heading in at maybe 15 knots.

If memory serves (from a day I'd like to forget), several custom rigs in the 65' range passed us. Even they were throttled back, running maybe 20 knots. By 4:45 we had crossed the bar and were heading for the bridge, then the channel. I stood up for first time in six hours and unsteadily got to a chair. I drank two bottles of water.

Well, at last, my lesson was learned. It turns out that a bucket can be used for many things. It can store bait, be used to transport trash, can scoop up water to clean the deck. It can also be a vehicle for a memory. A reminder of something that one should not forget… On days with 20 plus knot winds blowing or heavy weather expected, you will find me sitting at the dock with cold drink in hand…waiting to greet you and help with the lines! Lest I forget this lesson, all I need to do is look at a bucket.

THE DOCTOR AND THE BOAT

About 10 years ago, I was bringing a trailer of wild boars to the butcher. Mark from Mark's Meats, who happens to be the best butcher ever, was expecting me at a set time. As I arrive, I see a tall, thin guy sitting by the table. He was wearing camo.

Though he was there ahead of me, he agreed to wait until they got my pigs off loaded. I drive a Grand Cherokee, a decent sized SUV, but have pretty bad left knee, especially after a day's hunt. When the knee is acting up, I struggle a bit to get out.

Thin guy wisecracks, "You need a bigger car!"

I laugh and say back, "You oughta see me trying to get outa my Italian sports car."

He laughs back and says, "I think you're full of shit!" The butcher's wife, it turns out, overhears this exchange.

After a few minutes, thin guy looks at me and says, "You really need a Cortisone shot in that knee."

I respond, "Yep, I do. Are you gonna give it to me? Are you a doctor?"

Thin guy then says, "Yes, I am."

To which I say, "I think you're full of shit!"

By this time Pam, the butcher's wife, is cracking up! She continues to laugh as she says, "Doc, Jeff does have an Italian sports car and Jeff, Dr. Petrera is a very well-known orthopedic surgeon. He has five offices and an entire group of doctors working for him!"

Well, that was on Saturday. On Monday, he gave me the shot in my knee. He has since become, as the kids say, my BFF!

That coming summer we began to fish together often. He had

not been offshore much, mainly fishing inshore for stripers, blues, flounder, and the like. It didn't take long, however, for the offshore bug to bite him....hard. The boat search began.

Like many men of middle age who had not stayed in the market, Bertram was the gold standard. The 31' Bertram was legendary and Doc fell in love with the idea of owning one. He looked up and down the coast from Maine to Florida. In fact, it is likely that he looked at every one that came up for sale over a period of maybe eight months.

Being that I was the one who "contributed to his delinquency," I helped him with his search. We physically looked at several, but the requirements list was pretty solid. Most just did not stack up.

The criteria included having correct power, being basically original (read *not badly renovated*), and possessing a solid hull. We looked for the appropriate boat in which to invest in order to make it exactly what he wanted. Each one we saw, however, had issues... most had many issues.

About a year before, I'd met an older man with a 31 Bertram in my marina. His boat was a Bahia Mar (the original express boat), built in 1972. It was in near perfect shape. The boat had its original Bimini top and even its original old style radar pole.

Not only was it original in all the right ways, but it had been repowered with newer Yanmar 315 HP engines...the perfect weight and power for the boat. I introduced myself and admired the boat. While talking he noted that he didn't use it much and probably would soon sell it.

After maybe eight months of very serious looking at any and all 31s that came to market, I suggested that Doc consider the older man's Bahia Mar. Though Doc had been looking for a flybridge, rather than the express style of this boat, he thought he just might like it.

The next thing you know, it was off to the marina in search of the owner of the Bahia Mar. The boat was on the hard when we got there and it was love at first sight. We managed to track down the owner, who suggested a fair price. Doc and he shook hands. All we needed now was a survey.

Fast forward to the survey... It was performed by a friend of mine who, in my opinion, is the best surveyor around-- certainly in the Mid Atlantic. He climbed all through the boat-- checking everything and everywhere. We took her for a sea trial and checked every piece of electronics. It was an exceptional, comprehensive survey that took maybe four hours or more to complete. The surveyor was thorough. When the surveyor was done, he called Doc over to discuss. He was very serious.

Doc, who had not been through a marine survey before, was thrilled with his pending new toy. His joy turned to panic when the surveyor called him over. He and I listened carefully to the survey results!

There were indeed issues with the boat. Here is the complete list: one faucet handle had a broken piece on it, the shaft stuffing box needed to be tightened and two hoses only had one clamp instead of two. After Doc walked away, still trying to understand what exactly it all meant, the surveyor told me that he had just surveyed a brand new 75' Custom boat...with more deficiencies!

From that point, after the disbursement of much money and good taste, Doc has turned the Priceless into the finest example of a 31' that I have ever seen. Not only that, Doc has learned to drive and handle her like he has been at the helm since she was launched.

Confessions of a Boat 'Ho!

"Jeff is one of the regulars fishing Indian River. He might be on his boat, on our boat or running another boat, but in the deep every nice day. He may be 'driving the bus,' working the cockpit or staying out of the way. We even made him reel in a white one and be wire/gaff man one day last season."

- Captain Dan Devine, *Sea Flame*
62' Viking, Indian River, Delaware

I moved to a new marina in early 2001. It was fairly small, with maybe 200 wet slips and about as many in dry stack. Most of the marinas in my past had had serious fishing rigs; this one however had quite a mix of boats. My slip mates included everything from pontoons to big sportfish fully rigged out-- and everything in be-tween. There were nice ones and some held together with duct tape. Others were only kept afloat by multiple, overused bilge pumps.

Shortly after moving into the marina, I retired. I sold my last company and concentrated on fishing. I generally try to get out every day that the weather's decent (read calm).

I generally get to marina by midmorning and decide on whether to fish or not from there. Either option—fishing or not—is great. The marina has an exceptional bar/restaurant where everyone tends to hang out for lunch or drinks. The place has good food and better company.

Around this time, I had begun writing occasional articles for several fishing magazines and had become known around the marina as a result. Since my general schedule was very pretty predictable-- either fishing or having lunch at the marina-- folks often came by with a question or two. Generally it was easy enough...

I enjoyed this routine for several years. While the lifestyle suited me well, over the course of a few years, I realized that, in a weird way, unbeknownst to me, I had become a " boat ho" of sorts. It began in the normal, innocent way...

"Did I know of any freelance mates?" and "Are there any Captains around to help do this or that with my boat?"... the usual. Over time, it just sort of progressed. Either as a result of articles I had written in Fishing Magazines or because I was always around the marina, folks started to come to seek advice or help. And, as a result, I became a "Boat 'Ho."

Soon it began to be more routine. The following are just a few of the experiences...mostly good and all fun.

The 31' Bertram - As noted in an earlier story, a friend (Dr. Pat Petrera) purchased the boat of his dreams, Bertram 31' Bahia Mar. As he had little experience with bigger boats, I was happy to invest hours in helping him learn what and how to handle his boat. After burying the bow a time or two, overcoming fear of running within a mile of the beach and the need to run only in the center of the inlet, he's become a skilled boat guy. He became comfortable in most seas, learned to judge wind and currents and runs the Mid Atlantic canyons like a pro.

The Motoryacht - A new, midsize motoryacht arrived in a slip last year. Bringing the boat in were a hired captain along with the owner and his wife. Nice folks, we pass them on the dock often, but notice that the boat never moves.

Soon, a friend asks why they don't cruise. They finally admit that they are "concerned" about getting in and out of their slip. I get a call. After a half hour's discussion with the new owners, we come to find that their broker told them to only use idle speed in marina!

While in some instances this may probably be good advice, their boat acts like a sail. It is gas powered (therefore with less compression than diesel) with smallish engines and rudders that are very little. Hence, in idle the boat is at the mercy of any breeze at all.

Thankfully there was easy answer. All we had to do was teach him that he only has steerage with water running by the rudders, so do not be afraid to use throttles for maneuvering. Two hours with him at helm...now he uses boat regularly and is a happy camper.

The 34' Center Console – One day a friend asked me to fish. The trip would take place in November and we'd fish for tog (*tautog*, a tasty bottom fish that lives in wrecks, for the uninitiated). It would be a short run of maybe 10 miles. The weatherman called for an afternoon blow. It was just the two of us on board.

The fishing was good. Sure enough, the wind picks up and keeps picking up until it's a steady 25 knots, with gusts of maybe 30 or more. It's not pretty, so in we go.

As we approach the slip, I ask what he wants me to do, bow or stern lines, whatever. He turns to face me, looks bit shaken and says, "Will you take the helm? I'm afraid to dock in this heavy crosswind."

So, we change places. With some experience docking was easy enough with good power. We get tied up. As we get ready to leave, I have to ask, "What do you generally do in this situation?"

Answer? "I have not had to face wind as badly in past, so I would have tied up to end of dock till next day."

The Big Sportfish - A friend of mine has been fishing his 35' Center console for couple years-- with full time captain running it. Soon he wants a bigger rig, so he buys a fairly new 50' class battle-wagon. The boat is gorgeous-- fully rigged, full tower, everything... a top dollar rig.

A couple days after he gets his new ride, I get phone call. "My boat is in wrong slip, will you move it for me?" I agreed to help and headed to marina to meet the owner.

Stepping aboard, I took one look at the panel. The boat had a dozen switches and circuit breakers! With not a clue about what controlled what, I said "If you just start it, I'll move it to new slip. I just don't want to hit your switches."

The owner replied, "I have no idea how to start it!"

We both had good laugh and called the delivery captain. We fired it up and got her into the right slip.

There are many more, most in the same vein...all good fun. Marina life...

WHEN YOU GET INVITED TO FISH...

It was July of 2010 and the summer season was in full swing. The offshore action had slowed down but the inshore fishing was heating up. The flounder and sea bass were fairly thick, punctuated by especially good numbers on the coral beds and wrecks.

With offshore being slow, I found myself bottom fishing most days and doing pretty well. Being very retired, I fish most every calm day. I rarely have too much of a plan, I just fish the weather.

Bottom fishing off of the Delaware coast is not difficult if you, 1) have good numbers, and; 2) understand baits and presentation. Once you have the basics down, you can generally expect to have limits of four flounder per person in an hour or so. Then you can get back to the barn for cleanup and lunch. (By the way, I leave the dock at the crack of ten...am).

One midweek morning, I was getting ready to pull out when a dock partner and his wife and son invite me to go out with them. It is something that I'm happy to do. I bring my two rods, an out-rodder rod holder, my terminal rigs (two hook, high and low style with a sinker on bottom) and two packs of large Gulp baits-- one chartreuse and one red and white. Off we go aboard their nice, comfortable 34' Regulator. He says he has numbers and bait, no problem.

For the first hour, we're drifting blindly in the shipping channel. We caught a couple of shorts. I'm using my rigs with 10 Oz sinkers. My hosts are using squid and minnows with four ounce sinkers that hold bottom, but just. Their line is out at 55 degree angle. My 10 Oz keeps lines vertical thus baits tend to flutter and attract vicious strikes. Lots of bottom fishing folks use this technique.

Finally we move and head to better numbers. We target a small coral bed in 85-90 feet. I have limit in half hour. A couple of my fish are decent size, one is 22 inches. My hosts, however, have not added weight. Their lines are way out and are still deployed with the same squid baits.

After limiting out, I began catch and release. Finally the son says, "Dad, can I change to what he's using?"

Gruffly, Dad says, "Okay."

Within 15 minutes of the son using heavier weights, a high low rig, and Gulps and he's catching fish. Mom also changes...soon, she and son limited. Dad, however, has one keeper. Sticking to his guns (and four ounce weights), he is not a happy camper. Finally, by hour three, he comes around...and catches his fish—including a 24 incher, his personal best flounder to date!

The moral of the story is easy. Ask around, find out what is working and where is the best place to fish. Adding this openness to asking, with the willingness to try new things might make all the difference.

These folks fish five or six times a year. Now they get as much information as they can...and they catch lots of fish.

The Writer & the Deep Drop

Once or twice a year, one of the local outdoor writers comes out with us. Our objective is usually just a bottom fishing trip to provide him some material. (See story below). This past year, however, he asked specifically to join us on a tilefishing trip. Tilefishing is a bit different than your standard issue bottom fishing, for it involves deep dropping with jig rods and/or electrics.

One day, as soon as we found the perfect weather window, we set out. The crew for the day was the writer, my friends Steve, Shane, Dr. Pat (whose importance on the trip will soon be apparent) and yours truly. The morning was flawless... seas flat calm, with a light and variable five knot breeze. We took Steve's boat so we would be able to give our writer friend close attention. The run to our first drop was 65 miles.

The specific numbers we were going to fish are closely held by both Steve and myself. On my machine the spot is labeled "Fish Market"—in case you need a reason for the secrecy. We each only fish these numbers once a year, but it's been a sure thing. The spot sits in almost 500 feet of water and the bottom has structure. It's a "fish market."

The blueline tiles here are so thick and aggressive that they start attacking the jig way before it hits bottom. Miss the strike? No worries... they hit until you hook up! And the best part? The fish are big. We get fish over 20 pounds every trip with majority between 15 and 20. The fish run so big here in fact, I tried to set the world record in this exact spot... I missed it by 10 ounces, by eight ounces and by one ounce. I am still trying for the record, although after a couple hand cranks I often change to electric (which no longer qualifies).

After a nice run and uneventful run, we hit the numbers and everybody hooks up. Our writer is up forward next to Dr. Pat, we three remaining anglers are in the cockpit. We've all dropped deep jigs (850 gram jigs) and are all into fish. Its mid-morning (tiles bite best in bright sun). It's still flat and it's late August and hot. The temperature was hovering around 90 degrees, maybe a bit more.... but very hot.

All of a sudden, in the middle of winching his tilefish from the deep, our writer says, "I don't feel so good…" He no sooner utters these words than he goes gray and starts to fall backwards...into the bean bags we had moved forward. Doc grabs the rod before it goes over (thank you, Doc...it was a new Tallica two speed on a Connley stick).

As soon as he had stopped the outfit from plopping into the drink, he put both his rod and the writer's into rod holders and began tending to our fallen comrade. With lots of help, we get our guy under the T top, ice him down, and pour cool water into his system until he started feeling better. Relieved that our writer buddy was stabilized, we could relax a bit. He was feeling much better but he was unable to stand and very done fishing for the day.

After all of this, maybe 30 minutes or so had passed during our at sea triage, the writer tells us that he's better, and suggests, "Please finish fishing, I'll be fine." Heading back to the bow, Doc finds that both rods still have fish. He then proceeds to boat one, then the other! Go figure...

We then proceeded to limit out on bluelines quickly. The thought of trolling for a bit passed through our minds, but the weather turned bad and we headed for the barn. The ride home was a bit "sporty" but four of us managed to keep mostly out of the spray.

I was on the helm. The seas were now running four to five feet with a couple six-plus thrown in for good measure. We were running maybe 20 knots. This wouldn't sound like the most pleasant 65 mile run in the world for the four of us who were still vertical… It was even worse for our writer. The poor guy was flat on his back in the cockpit sprawled out on bean bags… getting drenched…all the way back.

Our writer friend had a tough day indeed. Being the trooper that he is, he actually wrote about it in his column. He has earned the deepest respect of our entire crew.

The Marlin Club

Truth be known, I have never been a "joiner". Aside from a stint playing football back in the day, I've always shied away from group things. Sure, I enjoy having a group of buddies and friends, but the organized part...not so much. Even when it came to sports... I always preferred individual activities like tennis or pool (billiards type) and the like. I always figured that organized club type deals would force me to be around too many chest-pounding types and to endure other things I didn't care to. While this perspective may indeed ring true in some instances, when it comes to fishing I was very wrong about this one!

One evening my wife and I were invited for dinner by my friends Mark and Pam Hess. Mark and Pam are members of the Ocean City Marlin Club and they suggested that we dine at the Club's restaurant. We agreed.

Not being big on the whole "club scene," I wasn't sure what to expect. In fact, I might have even had a reservation or two. Upon having dinner there, I could not have been more surprised.

The food was exceptional, the atmosphere even better. Mounts and fish pictures covered the walls...very tastefully. It was my kind of place. The building stood alone with beautiful view that overlooked the harbor. It was quite an impressive experience.

After dinner, still at work solving the world's problems, we decided to head to the bar. Upon getting to the bar, we were greeted by another pleasant surprise. Awaiting us was a huge, beautiful bar, attended to by friendly bartenders who served great drinks...at very reasonable prices.

We had no sooner bellied up to this beautiful bar before two couples came in and sat just to my left. One couple turned out to be Chris Evans and his wife. Chris is the son of John Evans, a close friend of mine. Chris is also the co-Captain of a well-respected local charter boat. Chris introduced us to the other couple, the man of the two happened to be the other captain of the charter boat.

Before you know it, we were consumed with conversation and sharing stories of fish and boats and captains. After a half hour of rousing talk about fishing and other topics, the other co-captain gets around to asking why I was not in the Club. It was then that I informed them my view on organized membership entities and fear of forced exposure to chest pounding and one-upmanship.

Upon hearing my long held reservation about this sort of thing, he very politely tells me that in the case of the Marlin Club I could not be more wrong! Chris chimes in as do Mark and Pam. After a period of conversation, I fold and agree that my hosts must indeed be correct. Never one to be accused of pandering to peer pressure, I try a few more "but this" or " but that"... before finally agreeing to apply for membership.

That night was maybe 10 years ago. The guy with Chris turned out to be President of the Club, Captain Franky Pettolina. Franky is a true gentleman for whom I have gained great respect as fisherman, a world class boat surveyor and an exceptional Club President.

What was the best part of that night? They were all correct. It turns out that this Club is fun. Not only does it host great social events and tournaments, but its membership is comprised of a wonderful group of men and women who are always willing to help each other, return calls on the radio. It's just nice. Yep, I could not have been more wrong!

Steve's (Winking) Blue Marlin

Steve is one of the guys with whom I fish often. He is an exceptionally good all-around fisherman. An airline pilot by profession, Steve approaches fishing with diligence and research. While Steve has caught almost everything out there, the blue marlin has eluded him....so far.

Fast forward to about a year ago. Reports surfaced that there were wahoo around the 30-40 line. Boats had been catching them fast trolling. Steve and I decided it was time to get into the action ourselves. We would put in around the 20 line, troll our way to the deep then switch to offshore rigs. Our hope of course was for a shot at a blue one. September in Delaware is often good for that sort of thing. We had a plan!

We deployed four fast trolling rigs. The crew worked the cockpit, I was at the helm. The water around the 30-40 line looked green and we saw almost no life...but this is where the wahoo had been caught, so we worked it hard.

We worked the 30 line mostly, in to the 20, and back to the 40. We were trolling maybe 12-13 knots and covered a lot of ground. We had no hits and saw no life in the green tinged water. Our outlook appeared bleak. As we worked our way to the 40 line, the water was still far from pretty and we were approaching mid-morning. Not one to waste our day "internet fishing" we decided to pick up and run to the 100 to try for billfish.

That's the picture. The only sensible thing to do is move. I pull back the throttles, get down to maybe three or four knots and the crew begin to bring in our trolling plugs. After reeling two into the boat, with the two remaining maybe ten feet behind the boat, it happens.

All of a sudden, maybe six feet off of the port side, a pointed dorsal slowly rises out of the water... Then the rest of the fish appears...it's a blue one! He's big, not huge but big...clearly in the 400 pound class... It was easy to gauge its weight as he swims right beside the boat in greenish tinged, 40 fathom water for a full 20 seconds or more! As this was going on, Steve and Shane desperately tried to find a bait (we still had big plugs on) to interest him. As they pillaged through tackle bags and the bait cooler, he slowly submerged... unhooked and unmolested peacefully back to the depths.

Given that my buddies were trying every which way to get a bait rigged, they definitely did not see him the entire time that he was beside us. My position at the helm, however provided me with the perfect vantage point to watch him the whole time. Although I didn't have the heart to tell the boys at the time, I am absolutely certain that he winked at us just before he slid away!

The Outdoor Writer
and The Bottom Fishing Trip

From the dock through the inlet, the ocean is no more than half a mile journey. A jettied inlet, the trip is an easy passage, one that never poses a problem. With the bottom fishing grounds pretty close (10-15 miles), trips of couple hours are often my norm.

Knowing all of these facts, my writer friend (who I like a ton and is central to another story here included), called one day to ask about my bottom fishing plans for the next few days. Given that my plans are often the same-- we go fishing if the weather warrants—I told him he was invited and to be at the boat around 10:00-10:15ish.

An excited and eager fisherman, we did a few minutes of the "Why so late? Why not dawn" discussion. No matter who is asking the question, or how they phrase their inquiry, my answer always the same. 1) I have coffee with my wife; 2) I take dog for walk, and; 3) Bottom fish do not wear wristwatches.

The next day we meet at 10:15. I fire up the boat and off we run to the coral beds (it's red soft coral off of Delaware). Our target fish are flounder (or fluke) with occasional sea bass in the mix. My guest has his go-to bottom rig... a light jig with 1/4 ounce white jig teaser 24" above it. We're fishing 85-90 feet, current pushing us at just under a knot. It's just about right.

Over the (many) years I have learned what for me is the best way to bottom fish this area, especially when it comes to the coral beds or rocky structure. We set up to drift starboard side forward by adjusting the direction of the motors. We then set two rods at 90 degree angles off the port side such that lines do not go under the boat.

The rods we use are fairly flexible sticks rated for 15 pounds, the reels are 12 pound outfits spooled with hi vis 20 braid. We equip the rigs with fairly heavy sinkers, in the 10 to 12 ounce range, such that lines generally stay mostly vertical. Our typical terminal rigs are hi and lo double hooks with six to eight inch soft plastics for bait (Gulp, Hogy, etc).

As we drift, the rods are set in rod holders. The game is dead sticking—you just watch the tips. At the slightest twitch, the very slightest, you drop back maybe three or four feet. From there, you lift up and 90 percent of the time you are hooked up.

On this day, fishing with my writer buddy, we had fished for an hour and twenty minutes. By this time, I have limit in the box (four over 18") and have released one more keeper sized flounder. My guest has one released short.

After our fill of floundering, we decide to pick up and try for trigger fish on a wreck. On our first attempt, we are greeted with no love. It is the same for the second wreck, not a bite. Looking down at my watch, the time is about 1:15—the time to get back to the barn.

For much of the day, my guest has been fairly quiet. He appears subdued. As we start to pack up, he looks bit puzzled. Before long, I have to ask about his reticence. He thinks for a bit, then says, "I guess maybe I'm not too old to learn. You and your friends do what I tell folks never to do... You don't work the baits, you let the boat do it... Then it's twitch, slight drop and hookup! It works really well!"

As we finish up, he adds, "And, I always thought that really fast boats were, well, foolish. But, today, we fished three widely separated areas. The seas were calm so we wasted no time running. I guess that's another thing to learn."

So, once again, to his credit, he later writes a long column expressing clearly how it is very important to be open to new ideas, new ways of doing things.

Three Dudes ... and a Beast!

Mid May 2009 ... a few years after retiring, still early for the yellowfin tuna blitz, early for flounder, but the boat is fully prepped and ready to go. Sea bass in season, but of no interest to me (full limit of 15 yields enough filets for two meals...maybe), yet weather great and seas calm and enticing. Over the last year or so, I've become friends with three of the local mates ... all young bucks, strong, dedicated and anxious to fish. Three dudes in particular are guys I really like, my wife calls them the "Boy Scouts" ... great guys!

So, on this particular nice day, we are hanging around the local tackle shop considering our limited options. The discussion gets around to shark fishing ... makos around but way offshore; the normal cadre of "blue dogs", bulls, spinners, etc, are catchable within a forty mile run, not much interest here either. But, this time of year finds threshers breeding fairly close in ... an easy eight mile run. And, along with makos, threshers are great on the table. So, threshers become the plan.

Heading directly East of Indian River Inlet for eight miles puts us at B buoy, the beginning of the separation zone for ships coming into Delaware Bay, just 15 miles up the the road. The bottom here is 75-90 feet, some structure, lots of dumped ballast stones over the years and fertile fishing for bottom fish within easy reach of the mosquito fleet. Six miles South lies A buoy, the entrance to the Shipping Channel. We plan our drift to begin at B and allow the outgoing tide to take us South toward A. Now, all we need are three 50's, 10/0 circle hooks on cable leaders, balloons, baits (bluefish filets) and a bucket of chum. We load up the boat (35' Center

Console) and begin our drift mid morning.

The boys set out the chum bucket and let it soak for ten minutes. The first bait is let out with a bit of weight, maybe 70' deep help up by a balloon. The second bait goes out, also weighted but maybe 35' deep, with balloon. As we begin to deploy the third bait, the surface rig ... the second bait balloon starts to move ... against the current ... and then disappears!

Mate number one takes the rod, gives a bit of dropback than starts to reel (circle hooks do not need a hard hook set) and hooks up! The fish runs a bit, than its tail hits the surface, clearly a thresher! The long tail is the giveaway! It was long for sure, but we (thought) we had a visual and called it maybe 150-200 lb range. No problem. Mate number one has the rod, puts his shoulder to it, tightens the drag to maybe 22-23 lbs ... and fights the fish. Thirty minutes go by, than an hour ... he cannot gain any line ... the fish is maybe three hundred yards out and as we work it with the boat, he keeps the distance between two and three hundred yards. Our angler gives it his best! But, the fish is in control. Our guy fighting standing up ... no harness. As we get to end of second hour, our guy gets tired, second mate takes the rod.

Pretty much the same ... the fish works us over, generally staying deep and couple hundred yards out ... but somewhat closer. We manage to keep the other boats away as the battle continues. Another hour goes by ... steady pressure on the fish ... and in the middle of hour four, our fish clears the water maybe a hundred fifty yards out. We gasp! Our medium sized thresher isn't! Our fish is huge ... a beast. We are in shock as we look at each other we do the inevitable " how big?" assessment. The boys look at me for a guesstimate ... we are all stunned. Trying not to overestimate, I call the fish 600 ... but, deep down, knew it was closer to 800 and maybe larger ... Beast! State record is 825 lbs ... this one close? Mate number two had already put the gloves on for wiring, turns to me and says quietly,

"Wow, boss man, this fish scares me, think you could wire it?"

So, the game has changed ... a lot. We settle in for long haul. Mate number two is still on the fish nearly two more hours. The fish is closer but no matter what I do with the boat, he keeps about a hundred yards out ... we close the gap, he opens it ... repeatedly. It's a standoff. We drink water, we snack, we work the fish ... we are gaining, but only slightly and in hour four going on five. Mate number two ... standup, no harness ... whipped. Mate number three now on the rod!

Another couple of hours go by...only change is we get fish within fifty yards, but once again, the fish determines the gap, not us. Nothing changes ... we work the boat closer, he moves away, tail whipping the surface to froth on occasion. It's clear though, our fish is not close to whipped. Beast! And in control.

Soon, we are at six hours on the fish ... all the while having planned on a quick run to catch and be back at the barn within maybe couple of hours. Fish still at fifty yards, still in control. We start to consider our options. There are not many. First option? Fight the fish from the rod holder? We discuss ... we know it's not going to qualify as a record given multiple folks on the rod, but we agree that, if we use the rod holder, the fish has won. Second option? Tighten the drag and give it the best we can ... full well realizing that this changes the odds ... from us to the fish, even more so.

We decide on option two. Our fish is on a 50W, spooled with new high quality mono, rod a Custom stick with soft tip yet heavy backbone ... yet we are all aware of the risks of tighter drag, the likelihood that out main line has been weakened by the fight, but the thrashing tail. We decide as a team ... let's tighten down, see if we can close the gap and maybe get close enough to wire and hit it with the the flyer. We all know understand the risk of this move ... it means we either take the fish ... or lose it! We agree.

Drag moved to 30 lbs, working fish with the boat ... we gain nothing. But, we are well aware of the need to either capture the fish or to break it off before it builds up an oxygen debt and dies in the deep. We add another three lbs of drag, we work closer with the boat, the fish moves away ... keeping the exact distance. He's still in charge!

Early into hour seven, fish still in control, fifty yards away. We move the boat closer yet, getting to maybe ten yards ... when our fish turns hard, runs off maybe another hundred yards ... as if he's never been hooked ... and the main line gives out just above the leader! Frayed? Yep, very much! He wins.

So, we stare at each other. It's another of those mixed feelings deals (like watching your mother in law drive your new car off a cliff) ... we really wanted to boat the beast, but we knew that he won, hands down. We have had a wonderful experience that we will carry in our memories, each in our own way.

Me? I had wonderful day with three great young guys, hooked a huge fish, fought it for hours and it won. Wouldn't trade the day, the experience for anything ...!

(Addendum: Several years later, while on helm of friends boat, we caught and boated a thresher ... see the picture. Caught on a 50, fought by one guy ... Shane ... for about two hours, weighed in at 400 lbs plus. Best guess? Half the size of the thresher that whupped us!)

THE PERFECT BOAT?

There is no perfect boat. There is a perfect boat for you, for him, for me, for her...but there is not one single boat that is perfect for everyone. It just ain't so! But, and there's always a "but," after more years than I will admit to, I'm going into the "Valley of the Shadow of Death"... in public... to offer an opinion.

First, it should come as no surprise that I am, and have been for years, enamored with the Carolina look. For me, there's just something about the "proud" bow and the entire range of custom rigs built along the Carolina coast. That said, the Florida custom builders, some of the New England builders-- almost all of the custom guys are fantastic. They just are!

I have been more than fortunate over the years to have fished on many, many boats...big and small. Some quality, some not so! To name a few, there were: Hatteras, Spencer, Davis, Omie Tillett, Bertram, Viking, Scarborough, Chris TF, Trojan (yep, I did fish on a Trojan), Harris, Formula-- the list goes on and on, really. Over the years there have been lots and lots of boats.

Over all of these years on the water, I've had plenty of time to reflect on the matter. If every boat is a compromise, what boat do I think is the best compromise of all?

To start with it helps to identify criteria: these are mine! (You'll likely have your own criteria, but these are mine.)

1. A boat should be big enough, but not so big slips are a problem.

2. A boat should handle well in various sea conditions. Handling in a head sea and a following sea are critical.

3. A boat should have the correct power. The metrics of note here are cruise speed, range and fuel efficiency.

4. A boat should have access to everything when needed, without taking the boat apart.

5. A boat should provide storage for tackle, for fish, for spare parts, and for everything else it needs to carry.

6. A boat should be comfortable for the crew, the captain and the guests. Consider the ease of getting around the bridge, the interior and cockpit.

7. A boat should be fully rigged with electronics and everything needed to be safe and comfortable.

Note: I purposely left affordability off of the list. Affordability is a standard that is as subjective as they come and entirely variable—differing greatly, sometimes even to people within the same tax bracket. Once you decide upon the affordability threshold that works for you, consider these criteria.

Guided by the list above, the optimal range of perfect boat begins to narrow. I default to a rig in the 60-ish range with cruise in 30-32 knot range. Lots of boats now fall out of the picture.

A boat of this size is large enough to travel just about wherever you want to go (if you use a yacht transport vessel, you could take a 60 foot boat to Australia for three seasons on the Great Barrier Reef and then bring her home). A boat of this class has enough storage and stateroom capacity to accommodate a captain and crew as well as the owner and a guest or two. It is not so big however that you'd need to worry about dockage or draft issues in most of the places that you're likely to take her.

A 60 or so foot boat also has plenty of fuel capacity and ample engine room storage for the spares needed for safe overnighters or extended passages. It also likely has plenty of cooler and freezer space necessary keeping food and beverages, bait, and if all goes according to plan lots of fresh tuna, dolphin and wahoo.

To me, the boat that best fits the combination of my criteria is the 62' Viking. One of the better rigs fishing out of Indian River is the *Sea Flame*. She's a 62' Viking 2018 owned by Rick and Andrew Levinson and Captained by Dan Devine. The hull is pure Viking. She is light gray, boasts a full teak cockpit and full mezzanine seating. Everything you'd expect in a Viking.

These guys have had several prior Vikings over the years and have incorporated some additional touches that truly make the difference. She is powered by twin C-32Cats at 1925 HP each. Loafing she's at 30 knots—that comes to 40 knots plus if you are in a real hurry. On the bridge sit triple Release Marine helm chairs and every bit of instrumentation you would ever want. Not only that, but she has extra hand rails for bridge access and a Release chair with rocket launcher in the cockpit.

The boat's interior is no less appointed. The salon island, dining area, refrigeration and staterooms are all top of the line. Even the TV in the salon—which rises out of and retracts into the counter, can either be a TV or a slave to the bridge electronics. By the way, the Seakeeper helps a ton, too!

In my humble, the ride is as good as one can get in the 50-75 foot range. Sure, this rig or that cuts a head sea better or that or this rig is less twitchy in following sea, but since one rig has to do it, all... this one gets my vote. It is a factory hull, with correct power, custom touches and everything you would ever want.

Every rig is a compromise. I vote for *Sea Flame* as the best compromise of which I am aware!

In Conclusion

Thank you, friends and foes, for taking the time to read this... it's my musings over years of fishing. The stories are all true, the characters as well, as best my aging memory serves. The typos, screw ups are all mine.

I have to extend grateful and heartfelt thanks to Elliott Stark, the editor of *In The Bite Magazine*, for his efforts to keep this project on track and his expertise in editing and composing. Without his help this would be a real mess! Far more than it is. And for what it's worth, do subscribe to the magazine, it's totally dedicated to us...the folks with fish and boats in our blood.

And of course, kudos to everyone who enjoys our sport and especially the fun and craziness that goes with it! Lastly, please do your best to support our local tackle shops. These local businesses offer help and information... things that are all too hard to find in this technology age.

- Captain Jeff Waxman

About the Author

Jeff Waxman is a lifelong fisherman whose affliction latched on early and never let go. With his wonderfully understanding wife Eileen, Waxman has two wonderful daughters and a three year old granddaughter. Capt. Jeff has owned many boats and was involved (fishing and owning a charter boat) in the Oregon Inlet fishing scene for decades. His wide ranging fishing exploits were supported by a successful career in technology, which saw Waxman serve as CEO of five network security companies that he would ultimately sell. Now retired, you can find Waxman, Eileen and friends in Delaware in the summer time and the Florida Keys in the winter. Jeff has a fishing rod in hand most days that the weather cooperates.

About the Editor

Elliott Stark is the Editor-In-Chief of *InTheBite Magazine*. A marine biologist, Elliott has traveled extensively-- working in billfish conservation, fishing (and writing about it), and running a marlin fishing lodge in Panama. Elliott began fishing as a child in Texas. His first "real" job was as a Science and Policy Specialist for the Billfish Foundation. To date he has fished on four continents and is one spearfish away from a billfish Royal Slam. He has two little girls and also enjoys hunting. Elliott operates Starkfish LLC, a boutique consulting firm with emphasis in writing, sportfishing and ocean-related enterprise and other ventures: www.StarkfishLLC.com.

www.ingramcontent.com/pod-product-compliance
Lightning Source LLC
Chambersburg PA
CBHW050844270326
41930CB00020B/3471